PREPARE TO BE TORTURED

THE PRICE YOU WILL PAY FOR DATING A NARCISSIST

By

A B JAMIESON

CONTENTS

INTRODUCTION

A damp dreich Friday night in early November in Glasgow's West end! A time of year that only Scotland knows best, in that no matter the layer of clothing, the dampness still manages to seep through to the bones. It matters little that it's now officially the run-up to Christmas.

Until the office party season kicks in, there's little incentive to do anything other than stay warm indoors. Apart from me, that is. If I'd known what I was letting myself in for, would I have still gone ahead with the date? Of course, I would. The year was 2009, and the date was the 17th of November.

We all remember the first times because they leave lasting impressions or indelible scars. Passing your driving test, first job, getting laid, first car, first house, and for anyone who's been on the wrong side of a narcissistic relationship, the first to inflict the kind of damage that leaves previous relationships positively inconsequential by comparison.

I was in my mid-forties by the time of meeting up, and with several relationships already under belt, why would I need to worry about the wool being pulled over the eyes. By this stage of my life, not a chance. Anyway, what was there to worry about? All the phone chats leading up to this point had been fluid and easy.

So much in common, albeit verbally, that it felt like we had already known each other for a lifetime! Her words were not mine, and why would I disagree. Tonight's date felt more a formality [she beat me to it with that one as well], but that was the thing about chatting with her into the wee small hours and running up a three-figure telephone bill in the process.

On just about every subject matter there was going, we just seemed to be on the same page. Again her...okay, you get the gist! Was she telling me what she really thought or what I wanted to hear? Hell, the former surely! I was a narcissistic dating virgin, so why would I possibly believe anything to the contrary. She came across as being so sincere that to doubt simply never crossed my mind.

So back then, what did I know about narcissism? Same as everyone else in that until affected, why would anyone bother to read up? With next to no coverage in the mainstream media, I had better things to do with my time than familiarise myself with the distant story of some Greek God who thought he was the greatest thing till sliced bread came along to steal his thunder.

When I was a kid in Glasgow, there was a saying mainly applicable to men who fancied themselves a bit more than most that 'if they were chocolate, they would eat themselves'. But it was spoken half-heartedly, and usually, the recipients were the self-deprecating types, so no offense taken.

It usually applied after being caught looking in the mirror a bit more than average in much the same way someone clocked the young Narcissus falling in love with himself upon seeing his reflection in the pool of water. The same principle, just the odd century or so of difference!

There were no criteria other than looks when it came to being labeled this way, but likely there would be a percentage who deployed the same modern-day characteristics. Just that I was too young and everyone else too naïve to know better!

Since becoming enlightened on the subject, it's now plain there have been many narcissists who featured in my life long before the partner of my dreams came along to act as the catalyst for what has become something of an obsession in recent years. Love interest narcissists do leave their legacy.

Had it been a blizzard instead of the November sheet rain, the date would still have gone ahead regardless, and no matter the scarcity of the fellow diner, I was oblivious to just about everything until the waiting staff made it known they had a home to go to much as we should too.

Since the inaugural date, I've never been back to that Restaurant, yet I had been several times before and been suggested by friends since, but I would always talk them around to dining elsewhere. I have visited the street itself a couple of times but only when passing through and no other option.

Not that the experience left me traumatized, simply uncomfortable with anything liable to trigger a memory left well alone. The thoughts don't linger, just a nasty habit of ruining what was left of my day.

Narcissists leave their mark. I was never the life and soul type but at least amenable to engaging with just about anyone who crossed my path. It's since been pointed out by a close friend and the occasional work confidante that it's obvious I only ever allow people to get so far before the drawbridge gets wound up and after that a distance.

I am wiser rather than scarred. The journey since being taken in and spat out when a better offer came along, and subsequent manipulations during and after being dumped have sharpened the antennae for narcissist detection, and above all else, how to deal with it effectively.

Understanding why we allow ourselves to be taken in and messed around is as important as having an effective strategy and strength of character to deal with. It's in a narcissist's nature to push their luck, but they only ever get away with what we allow.

No one out there has a divine right to mess up a person's life or take advantage of their better nature without experiencing some kind of consequence as a result. The most effective punishment for a narcissist is also the easiest, and that is to ignore. This book intends to alert you to the way these people operate and, by definition, what to expect should you find yourself snared and initially unable to break free.

Narcissism is on the increase. Of that, there is no question. When I started on my quest to understand the whys and wherefore's of this uncharted territory, there were but a dozen or so books available on the subject, which nowadays run well into the hundreds. Draw your own conclusions as to why.

Dating narcissists can be fun, but the entertainment comes at a price that takes some of us years, if not longer, to recover from. I have tried to write this book in the context of the one I wished I'd had available a decade back when a helping hand was needed the most. If you happen to be standing in my old shoes, it's my sincerest wish that the picture becomes more evident that much quicker than the process I had to contend with. I wish you well.

CHAPTER 1

THE IDEALISATION PHASE

There are dates to look forward to and dates to get excited about, and this one is definitely in the camp of the latter. One of those in a million moments when half-hour into the conversation, you are already planning your wardrobe in anticipation of the invite to come, and by the time the canapés are on their last legs, he has duly obliged.

'So tell me, would you be free for dinner sometime?'

Eh, is the Pope a Catholic?

'Sure, why not,' you duly reply, trying to play it low-key but no doubt failing miserably in the process.

'When did you have in mind?'

Not what you expected from yet another party invitation grudgingly accepted, but what's not to like about the kind of man that makes a terrific first impression. Self-confident, assured, and interesting! My god, what a refreshing change from tolerating yet another one of the world's hundred and one most predictable chat-up lines! You feel challenged, invigorated, alive!

Not that you are desperate, far from it. Still turning heads, but being on the wrong side of forty, maintenance and upkeep now take that little bit longer, and at some point, mother nature and gravity will soon take their toll. Caught up in that grey area of still having time on your side, but somehow birthdays come around quicker than they used to.

There is an exchange of telephone numbers before the parting of the ways, and mutual dialogue quickly ensues. Even your teenage daughter has noticed the latest spring in the step when the phone rings each night at bang on nine o clock.

You're eager to spread the good news and start telling friends about your fantastic new man. They urge caution. You do have a reputation for diving in headfirst, remember, but heh, what's to lose? Nothing ventured, and all that, and so the first date is set for one of the city's more fashionable restaurants.

You are first to arrive, and he follows after that in his rather plush seven series convertible. He comes across as a man of stature. The profession was yet unknown, but as he said at the cocktail party:

'In many people's eyes, I'm a success, but for me, it's just a means to an end. Money certainly isn't everything.' Certainly different from the majority, whose job titles are part and parcel of their predictable chat-up repertoire!

The meal goes as planned. Well, you knew it would from the moment he pulled out your chair. Good old-fashioned manners always tick more than one box. The conversation seems effortless with no nervous pauses.

He is open and frank about past mistakes without coming across as bitter as previous dates seem to have had this nasty habit of not being able to have moved on in their lives. You laugh about shared trials and tribulations, and then before you know it, you are at the coffee stage. Heavens, when was the last time that happened? The evening over and ever the gentleman he walks you to your car. With the next date in the bag for the following evening, the night ends with a gentle kiss on the lips. Time enough to inhale his intoxicating aftershave.

A twenty-minute drive home and pray to god the lights are all on green as the euphoria of the evening just has to be shared with two of your closest friends. Understandably they are delighted. That is when they manage to get a word in edgeways. 'Just go easy,' they say, a piece of advice you find mildly irritating, but you're a people pleaser, and you [and they] know you've had your fingers burned in the past. But nothing can spoil your mood.

Tonight there was something there. Chemistry, a connection; call it what you like. It just felt different. One of those rarities is when you feel as if you've known someone all your life! What was it your mother said at the last heart to heart? 'It'll happen when you least expect it'. It looks like, for once, she may have been right!

Sorry to burst your bubble, but your foot has just been placed on the bottom rung of the narcissist's relationship ladder. Tonight you will sleep like a baby, and this will continue for a few months yet. Longer-term, you may find yourself counting an awful lot of sheep.

This is the part your consummate narcissist does so well. The art of the great first impression. Like any other master craftsman, the skill has been honed and perfected over the years. It's no coincidence that so many narcissists work in media, sales, and marketing.

In these industries, image is everything, and they develop the tools to sell themselves very effectively. They are usually well-groomed, smell nice and drive nice cars. Throw in some charm, a healthy sprinkling of charisma, and heh presto, you've found yourself a great catch. So much so that you forget to ask yourself why they are still single but more on that later.

It's early days, so even the most ardent of narcissist spotters might still get taken in. However, its benefit of doubt syndrome primarily lets them off the hook.

You are like a whirling dervish when you sweep into the office the following day.

'Heh, what's with you? Have you won the lottery?'

'No, no, just in a good mood. How are we all this morning?'

∽

By the coffee machine, the glow has not gone unnoticed. 'Looks like someone had an eventful night last night, lucky bugger.'

You leave the mobile on your desk just in case, and by lunchtime, the waiting games are over.

'Are you free for lunch? Xx'

Sure you are. Safe to say, by lunchtime, you could be ravenous in more ways than one.

So the half-hour extends to an hour but still feels like fifteen minutes. Why does the time just seem to fly by with this guy? With a time already arranged for tonight's meal, it's a foregone conclusion what's in store afterward. Maybe not so much chat as it's about time you had some fun.

So it continues. The first week is a whirlwind. The second is a dream, and before you know it, a month has passed in the blink of an eye. Just being in his presence is beginning to make you feel differently about yourself. He has a certain aura and charm, and somehow he manages to make you feel good about yourself, putting things in perspective when life feels chaotic.

Everyone approves. Your daughter thinks he's pretty dishy for a man of his age, and your friends say you make a great couple. His height and grooming make him stand out, and you are only too aware of the admiring glances he can attract from other female diners. By judging by his attentions thus far, you feel supremely confident that his eyes are fixed firmly on you.

Two months later, you have your first weekend away in a country manner, no less. He definitely has a romantic streak, and there are flowers in the suite upon arrival. When has that ever happened before? It's been decided that this will be a tell-all, no holes barred, no stones left unturned type of weekend.

Your own story is relatively straightforward. One failed marriage, a teenage daughter whose fondness has been heightened by his promises of professional driving lessons. She has a relatively secure job, ten years left on the mortgage, and the odd pension deficit to correct.

He's a tad more complicated. Two ex-wives, even though you are sure he only ever mentioned one. Actually, he did only mention one, but it's a test to see if you let him away with or pick up on. If the former, it means you're not one for confrontation. Always a bonus!

The first wife left him for another man when they were only in their twenties. It's a classic case of marrying too young, and nothing abnormal about that: if you accept his account, the second comes across as a nastier piece of work with various issues, the frittering away of their cash being one of them.

Continual arguments over her reckless spending and flawed temperament meant the marriage had been on the skids for years. The resultant two divorces alongside ongoing child maintenance have placed a hefty burden on him financially.

Still, you are assured that the outgoings are easily covered with a job as an offshore financial consultant. Not that you're quite sure what the grandiose title actually means, but it sounds important, and narcissists are very good at dressing things up.

On top of this, there's been another child from a relationship outside the second marriage which he admits was his moment of madness, but it came at a time in his life when he just needed companionship. He has no contact with the mother now other than meeting his financial obligations. At the back of your mind, you're sure he mentioned this relationship minus it producing a child but it's a fleeting moment quickly forgotten.

Narcissists invariably come to new relationships with a] an unfortunate previous history where predecessors were either bitches from hell or wife beaters and b] no money because of a]. The more these tales go unchallenged, the greater the confidence in the latest candidate is an absolute pushover. Still, details get overlooked when one of the partnerships cries out for this relationship to have traction. Mainly the truth!

‿

The weekend seems to have drawn you even closer. Lazy mornings in bed, long walks in the countryside, romantic meals, and passionate sex that somehow seems to last all night.

You cannot help but fall for this man. He's been entirely open and frank enough to admit his failings, even if he's been a bit sketchy when it came to some of the numbers. Maybe that's just management consultants for you. You feel as if there is a natural empe that can look good, then you'll damn well make sure you do too. You've told him you're a keeper.

Another weekend away is suggested, and you jump at the chance. He is going to take you on that trip to Paris he has been promising at one of the city's finest hotels, no less. You are beyond excited and treat yourself to some designer clothes and sexy underwear for the occasion.

Not working out quite as expected, instead of the Ritz, you have to settle for a three-star along a backstreet well away from the sights, which he explains away as being entirely the fault of his secretary. He just left the booking to her given time constraints, and if only he'd checked to make sure, then none of this would have happened. But still, he flatters your new wardrobe to such an extent that the pain of missing out on staying at the capital's finest is soon forgotten.

Things finally begin to settle down. You are still trying to spend as much time together as possible, but he has commitments. He's not just your soul mate; he's your rock. Sure he's not perfect. There was that embarrassing incident at the restaurant when his credit card was refused. He did seem to berate the waiter a bit more than was absolutely necessary, and at times he can be a bit aggressive when driving. But with so much on his plate, is it any surprise?

Sometimes you think he may be a bit too eager to please, but you assume that's down to the extent of his love. He's also prone to exaggeration, but we're all guilty of that at times, indeed, and it's bound to self-correct. There's been the odd tiff but nothing major. Always resolved by applying the mantra of your parent's fifty-year marriage, never let the sun go down on an argument.

You are easy-going and like to please, a trait that your narcissistic partner picked up on a while back, and just the type that they tend to take to the proverbial cleaners. The small matter of moving in together has been broached on several occasions, mainly by him, and you admit you are tempted. He seems very keen, and it does make financial as well as emotional sense. Your daughter is less enthusiastic, and your friends agree. They say it's all a bit too soon, but still, he persists. His house is certainly big enough, if a bit spartan.

'It's crying out for the feminine touch,' he suggests.

Who could have foreseen all this in just the space of a few months? You are in love and utterly besotted by one of the best-looking guys you have ever clapped eyes on.

Did you ever see this coming?

Let me ask that question again. Did you see this coming? At any point, did it feel as if you were being lured into a spider's web? Slowly but surely coerced into a trap with no means of escape. Sure doesn't feel like that, does it?

It never does, I'm afraid. You don't know yet that the trap has been sprung, but you soon will, and to your high emotional cost.

What was it that made you so appealing to this man in the first place? Well, you're single, you're free, and you are attractive. All highly desirable qualities for a male partner! Better still, you're a nice person, sociable, gregarious, and caring. But even better from the narcissist's perspective, if it comes across early on that you are something of a people pleaser, the word that flashes in front of their eyes is VULNERABLE.

Where an average person sees touching vulnerability, a narcissist sees a golden opportunity. Remember, you are in the presence of a master manipulator. He has set out to seduce you and make you fall in love with him. He does this partly by picking up on the subtle clues that escape in the course of conversation and reflecting them in your direction. Essentially, creating a mirror image of the person you think you are, we all know how much like attracts like.

While you think you are having a normal two-way discussion, he is picking up clues as to your preferences, desires, and dreams, and he will use all that information to give you what you want. The person you think you know and love does not exist. He has molded himself into the person you want him to be.

In addition, and, most crucially by now, you have given him all sorts of clues about your weaknesses to be used against you later. The main weakness he has seized on is your vulnerability, your desire for love. We all want to be loved, just that some crave it more deeply than others. People like this are left wide open to emotional manipulation. Sure make a narcissist's task a whole load easier.

The meeting point doesn't have to be a particular social event. It could be anywhere but rest assured the narcissist is always on the lookout for a potential conquest's weak spot. If you are strong, assertive, and self-confident, the narcissist will not touch you with a barge pole. Why would they?

There is no pot of gold in that scenario. No, what they are looking for is a sign of weakness, an unlocked door that will lead to greater rewards on the other side. This is where you stand at the moment, the door slightly ajar waiting to be completely prized open.

Everything is fine just now. The future is rosy as you are attracted to this man like a moth to a flame. Unfortunately, he knows it. There is still a chance to escape before the going gets tough. Maybe tell him to cool it a bit. But taking things slowly is not the modus operandi of a narcissist. He sees himself through your eyes, and the love you give out means power and control for him.

If you can't help yourself, if the love you feel is all-consuming, then very shortly, you will be tested.

Because what you have been going through these past few months is the Idealisation phase of a narcissistic relationship. A four to six month idealization phase appears to be the norm. It is the all-consuming, coming at you from all angles, winning you over stage.

How could any woman stop herself from falling in love with such an attentive, charismatic, and good-looking man? Some might, mainly those fortunate enough to be focused on fulfilling their own needs. But unfortunately for you, you dropped your guard and are now in the narcissist's icy grip. The upcoming test will confirm what he thinks he already knows. The time feels right for him to go full steam ahead.

The test can have only one of two outcomes.

Either you will have the strength to walk away feeling a bit foolish and licking your wounds. Or, as he predicts, you will now conform to the pattern he has laid out for you and bend to his will.

The choice is yours, and it's coming real soon.

CHAPTER 2

THE DEVALUATION PHASE

It was only to be expected after several months that the frequency of texts and phone calls would begin to ease up, but somehow in the back of your mind, you always feel as if it's down to you to keep up the momentum. Or are you just being paranoid? He has repeatedly said, you think too much!

He used to always reply within minutes. Now it seems to be a good while later. If indeed that day! There's always a valid reason, of course, usually work or family, but to give him credit, he is a man who seems to be juggling lots of balls that you accept and make allowances for.

But still...something's niggling away. It just doesn't feel the same. You can't quite put your finger on it. He can be quite taciturn, and the moods seem to last longer than most, leaving you perpetually wondering if he feels this relationship is actually worthwhile. He used to be so affectionate. Now at times, he feels distant as if his mind is elsewhere.

What you don't realize is that the testing has begun in earnest. This is the 'Now let's just see'...phase. He sets a test. Arrive late, forget to reply to a call—the tests can take many forms, all of which involve him indulging in bad behavior.

If you accept that bad behavior, he sets another test, slightly trickier. He may fail to turn up to an agreed date or cancel an arrangement at the last minute. If you have any sense, you will kick him into touch. If you don't, he has won.

He now knows you can be poorly treated and will accept it so that he will continue in that vein.

Testing accelerates when, a short while later, you dare to ask if there's something wrong as he appears even moodier of late. This results in him snapping back that you don't appreciate his circumstances and how difficult things are for him.

Unusual for him to turn on you like this, as being relatively quiet and gentle is a considerable part of his appeal. He always said he hates melodrama. You backed off, even felt guilty, and apologized. But in truth, he can't believe his luck. The 'control' part of the equation is right on schedule. The deal-breaker might come even sooner than he anticipated.

'Hell, I'm good,' he thinks to himself. Here I am behaving like a complete idiot, and not only does she let me away with it, she still comes back for more. 'How good am I.'

You have always prided yourself on your self-respect. You'd have shown this guy the door in previous times, but unfortunately, you are invested in this relationship, and the emotion is ruling your heart and head.

That same evening you have a pre-arranged night out, and predictably enough, he is quiet and sullen on the drive there. On arrival, chameleon-like, he morphs into a different character. The minute the door opens, it's show time. The party's life and soul and crucially for him, and he wants everyone to see just how much of a great couple you have become. More tactile than ever, embarrassingly so and incredibly touchy-feely, showing you off to as many of his friends as possible, some of whom seem to pay deference for the privilege of being in his company!

He calls you 'Darling' a bit too often for your liking, and you feel like you are on display. But, on the other hand, this might just be his moment of glory, and who are you to burst his balloon! Mobile photo's a plenty which he seems to relish, and when the opportunity arises, he makes sure his arm is firmly around your waist, at one point even insisting a picture be re taken as he wasn't quite ready.

Perfectionist personified, but he has to get these pictures just right for posting on his social media profiles later on. It is an excellent opportunity to show his exes how deliriously happy he is in his new relationship. Some appropriate comments like 'soul mate' and 'don't think I've ever felt this way about someone' will also not go amiss! His exes see the pictures and think, 'ho-hum,' there he goes again, mentioning how deliriously happy he is! Poor woman, if only she knew what lies ahead'.

But a great night, and you are slightly in awe at the way he works the room, always seeming to have the right line for the right person at the perfect time. You quickly forget the embarrassing tiff earlier and, judging by the look in the eyes of a few single females in attendance. So, you should maybe just be counting your blessings after all. But, don't become too forgiving just yet, and the night is but young!

Driving home the first ten minutes is amiable enough. But for all his bravado and showmanship at the party, the insecurities still come out. Not so much a discussion on the party, more an analysis of his performance there. Were his stories the right length, did this or that joke go down as well as he thought, and even to the point was anyone else wearing as expensive a jacket as his! Best agree, you are tired, mentally, and getting into bed has never seemed more inviting.

But wait. It is time for a further test.

'Have to get this off my chest, darling but did you really have to go ahead and flirt with that younger guy when I only left you alone for ten minutes!'

What? Where did that come from?

'Don't give me that. I saw the signals that women give out, running your fingers through your hair, laughing at his every word. How do you think I felt.'

Is this guy for real?

You look at his face. He seems to be talking, half in jest, half contempt.

You blow up.

You defend yourself as best you can, but, composed as ever, he continues the onslaught, disappointed and hurt that you could behave like that.

Emotionally worn and annoyed by this nonsense, you decide it's best if he just drops you off and doesn't stay. Parking up, little but enough is said. You still kiss him goodnight, though, before he drives off. A wry smile comes over his face. Gotcha!

Exhausted but still going to be a long sleepless night.

Two texts were received. The first is from your daughter.

'Hi mum, hope u had a gr8t nite. Am a bit drunk! Luv yu xxxxxx

And the second.

'Sorry, but I can't help myself being jealous. I never knew I could love someone so much! Xxxxxxx'

Back home, you slide into bed while across town he puts on the telly!

You think to yourself, perhaps it's time you called it a day, but he does seem to have gotten under your skin.

That's what Narcissists do so well. They look for and find the gaps in your emotional well-being before seeping through and zipping up with no means of escape. The intention is to control and leave you adrift from the kind of friend who, unlike you, actually can see the wood through the trees.

Lying here in the darkness, you are in turmoil. On the one hand, you cant help but feel you are being used [of course you are, but that becomes more blatant later], but on the other, you can't stop thinking of him, and the more you see him, the more your heart melts. You haven't replied to his text, but by god, you want to.

Worse, you want to call him, and, hell, you just wish you were with him right now. The way he puts his arm around you in bed and squeezes you, drawing you close, your body just seems to fit into the contours of his. Tonight of all nights, you want him so much.

Were you flirting with that younger guy? Maybe it could have seemed that way to a bystander, but perhaps he was just a young cocky guy doing his best to impress an older woman. Christ, he could have been my son! How could he be jealous over that?

But...does that not just go to show how much he loves you after all. Thank heavens tomorrow is Saturday, that lunch date with the girls and some straight talking as only women know-how.

The kind of friends who tell you what you need to know but don't necessarily want to hear! So far, they all seem to like him. There is no indication that anyone has any reservations. So maybe you should see more from his perspective. But, oh, it is all so confusing. Your adolescent daughter will also be back, and if she had a cross to bear with anyone, you would be the first to know.

Is missing someone so much the same as being in love? He monopolizes your thoughts, and the hours go by like minutes when he's inside your head. This will be a restless night, and you are determined not to reach for the phone. Instead of counting sheep, you repeat the words 'don't give in...'

From his end, this is a disaster.

No texts or calls, and she hasn't replied to his. Damn, panic mode, time to revert to Chapter one, works every time.

By the time Saturday morning suburbia comes to life, you hear the key in the door, too early for your daughter surely and the footsteps heavier on the staircase. He's here, letting himself in with the spare key you had cut specially but surprisingly not reciprocated.

With a gentle knock on the half-open door, he probably knew you would be awake anyway. He looks good, casually dressed but still color coordinated all the same, and he's certainly had more sleep than you ever did.

'I thought you might like breakfast in bed, albeit in polystyrene containers,' from which you just about manage a half-hearted smile.

'I felt terrible about the way it ended last night [lie], and I cant count the number of times I wanted to come round to apologize [lie], and I'm here to make amends [half lie] to show you how much you mean to me [lie again].'

And so it begins again. He has tested you. This time you passed was a fail for him, and so begins the charm offensive all over again.

But as soon as you have fallen for this, he'll be back to his old tricks.

Oh god, lunch with the girls, and you had promised to take your daughter shopping afterward!

'Darling, that's the trouble with you. Always putting other people first. Listen, your daughter will probably be too tired after partying all night, and it always seems to be you that does all the organizing with those girls, so come on, give yourself a break, some 'me' time [when he says 'me' he means himself not you] and let's spend the day together. 'I'm going to spoil you because I seem to be the only person out there who really wants to!'

Awwww! Your daughter's not due back till after 12, and he smells so bloody insatiable that maybe just this once.

Then the inevitable...

You think this is proper lovemaking.

He thinks free sex and all for the price of a few well-rehearsed lines and a cheap takeaway. Hell, I'm good!!

You call the girls and leave a note for your daughter.

And so Chapter 1 is well and truly revisited.

Narcissists will always stick with what works, and what works for a woman in love is praise, flattery, and attention. He will get you back up on that pedestal and make you feel you belong there and no one else comes close.

By the end of the day, you wonder how on earth you could have doubted him. He genuinely feels so full of remorse—even time to talk about the future with the lure of what's still to come.

The word 'promise' will be used by him rather a lot now. It is a case of him working out what you want to hear and delivering those lines.

'It's about time we had a romantic holiday, somewhere exotic and...he's been thinking, how do you feel about living together?

It kind of makes sense when you think about it, pointless having two homes when you could move in with him, and there are two spare rooms for your daughter to choose from.

You could easily rent yours out and use it as an investment for the future. My god, he must love you to come out with this stuff. He does have a point. Neither of you is getting any younger, and if it doesn't happen now, it's not likely to occur in the future.

This should be viewed as a temporary respite. You are being deluded into thinking the blip was just part and parcel of settling down together. He is also taking advantage of your desire for love and your slight nervousness about being alone. This is what narcissists do so well. They identify your weak spots and take full advantage.

He goes out of his way to see even more of you, taking you to and from work even though you actually like the drive 'Darling, it's on my way, I really don't mind,' and you are now seeing even less of your friends, some of whom he has begun to rubbish, odd since he doesn't know them. But heh, it's the annual summer girls' day out next week, so you'll have bags of time for catching up on everyone's news and spilling the beans on how things are progressing on your end.

But bad news, a couple of days before you meet the girls, he declares he already had something else arranged for the pair of you, and you knew all about it. You are taken aback, and you are sure it's the first you had heard of it and nothing in your diary or Calander!

He seems taken aback once again in his very controlled matter of fact but demonstrably hurt kind of way. So this is it 'The Biggie', the Master's Degree of tests, your Tutor has decided its time, and a fail for you is a pass for him so let's proceed.

The body language is akin to the prosecution addressing the jury in its closing arguments. Palms of hands open, eyebrows lifted, and a slightly quizzical look on his face in a 'How is this possible' kind of way—a lethal cocktail of doubt, pleading, and control.

'Surely you must remember what I've organized, have you any idea how much this has cost me'? 'How could you be so inconsiderate...I can't believe you at times. I really cant!'

From that, the sermon moves onto how he feels like he is just being used and how you cannot keep disappointing him... adults don't behave this way...and it will go on ad nauseam.

This is narcissistic projection at its finest, projecting onto you so that you feel like the bad guy.

Nothing could be further from the truth, of course, but this is the test he's planned, and he needs to see how you handle it.

A shouting match ensues, of course, because that's exactly what he wanted. Remember what he once told you 'the person that loses control loses the argument, and you have to stay in control,' and control is everything for the narcissist. Of all the times to forget that crucial piece of advice!

It is worth noting you will always be on the defensive in any argument, and he will always be two steps ahead of you purely because he has carefully planned for all eventualities, and you have to think on your feet. Not your strong point.

God, this is so tiring. But he keeps coming at you with the emotional blackmail, and you are uncaring, unappreciative, and worst of all, manipulative!

What! That you will not take so, with a pointed finger just a millimeter from his eyeball and veins in neck swelling by the second.

'Just forget it,' he says, 'If this is how we are reduced to behaving, then I may as well go home!'

You retort, 'Well fuck off then—Go!'

Within seconds of him leaving, you break down. But all he has to do now is wait, and narcissists are very good at waiting, patient opportunists who only strike when the moment is right.

While you reach for the drinks cupboard and contemplate resurrecting your disgusting smoking habit, let's consider your options. Breathing space if you like before you crawl under the duvet and pray for the night to end.

There are two scenarios. Unless you have been surfing websites dealing with narcissism, you will be unaware of both.

The first is to believe that underneath all this nonsense, this is the man for you. This will result in the following.

You will simply become a shadow of your former self. Your life will unconditionally revolve around and be dependent on his. Your decisions then become his decisions, your friends will be discarded at his behest, and those retained will only be so for a reason. His decision, not yours. Your sole reason for being is to provide him with the support necessary to prop up his fragile self-esteem.

More often than not, you will also be the required punch bag that takes the blows when things don't go his way. You have unwittingly already become a punching bag, so it's just more of the same, albeit with greater ferocity. Should you ever dare to stand up for yourself, this is when the torture begins, mental then possibly physical.

You will be reminded of how meaningless your life was before you met, how you are boring, unintelligent, and unable to survive without him. Physical violence when mental torture has been exhausted is not uncommon. It might be a good idea to learn self-defense under the guise of taking evening classes in cookery 'because darling, I want to become an even better cook just for you!'

The second and more tortuous scenario, because now you are in love, is simply to walk away.

But will he let you? Rejection hurts any person, but it practically kills a narcissist. If you walk away, rest assured he will revert to Chapter 1 until you are entangled once more. All the while, ironically, he will have started Chapter 1 with someone else as Narcissists tend to get bored very quickly, so best have someone in place for when your shelf life comes to an end.

Either way, you are toast, but best be toasted on his terms as that's better for his ego. All the stuff he told you about his ex-wives being deranged, well, I hate to tell you, but he will now be telling his latest conquest that you too belong on the same boat.

This is the hypocrisy of narcissists. They can lie to you, steal from you, and cheat on you, but you can never leave them because that's not fair, and if you do have the gall to go, rest assured they will try their damndest to stay in your head one way or another.

They will leave voicemails when they know you're not at home, turn up at restaurants they know you frequent, that kind of thing. The object is to keep you off balance and thinking about them.

Eventually, they get the hint, but it requires much strength from you, and the words with one syllable are mostly found on building sites and playing fields.

Of course, you could end up being friends, but friendship for a narcissist bears no relation to the standard definition. Narcissists do not have friends for friendship's sake, but they need people like the rest of us to need oxygen to survive.

But they think their fellow man is there simply there to be used. The greater the use, the higher the value they place on the 'friendship'. In professional terminology, this is generally defined as Narcissistic Supply, where people provide a continual source of affirmation and attention, giving the Narcissist a regular fix to their fragile sense of self.

So can you be friends? Well, yes, but if the narcissist already has lots of attention and admiration, you will be well down their list of priorities.

Much better from the Narcissists perspective if you are of some social standing, wealthy, are attractive, and can regularly organize events because then you serve their purposes and are of use from which the narcissist can attend [for free of course] and once again give the kind of performance that makes them the center of attention.

For sure he thinks 'great friend' to have whereas normal people will think 'freeloader'! Charming, courteous, and appreciative when things are provided, but ask the favor to be reciprocated, and they are gone in the blink of an eye.

Rest assured, if you remain friends and one way or another, a loose friend on his terms is all you will ever become anyway you are only there for one reason and one reason only, to be used, be it free sex or free handouts. As for a shoulder to cry on, forget it, he has already moved on to swooning his next victim to provide the emotional stuff!

So back to the here and now.

As expected, the phone lines are red hot—two opposing schools of thought from closest confidantes. The first is the slightly rose-tinted version from a friend happily married to her childhood sweetheart for twenty years.

She summarizes that although he is a charming, charismatic man, he has insecurity issues, which you need to work on together. Don't worry. He'll come round. Look what he has to lose! How could any sane man possibly give up someone like you? Give him time, reassure him, let him learn to trust you in his own time, and you will keep him forever.

Hmmm, rose-tinted right enough and big on forgiveness!

The second takes a more pragmatic approach. Having kissed a few frogs in her time, her bullshit detector antennae have laser-like sensitivity.

'Wake up and smell the roses, for god's sake! There's been something about him from day one, but I never felt the time was right to mention it. All that crap about being hurt, seeing you flirt, well, seeing as I was there, I can tell you he was doing a fair bit of chatting up himself when you were not in sight, and I could see for myself you were engaged in conversation with a nice harmless guy. He seems to have a selective memory. And is it me, or does he like hogging the limelight a bit too much and talk about singing your own praises! We never see you anymore, and you always seem to have to ask his permission to do things. When we get together, it's as if you always have to hurry home if he's upset. Are you in a relationship with a grown man or a five-year-old? How long have you known him, and this is what he's like already! What's your life going to be like a few years down the line?'

As for my daughter, she is no longer a fan! 'Why do we have to move in with him, he only lives up the road, and he's a right moody shit. I know when he's here because I feel the atmosphere when I open the front door like I've got a cheek being in my own house. I thought he said he would help me with my driving lessons? He keeps making promises but never keeps them. Hate to say it, mum, but I don't like him anymore!'

But all that said, you know you cannot bear to have this man leave your life. If you just keep doing what you do, he'll realize he would be a fool to give you up. You wish he would call, but it's not even been twenty-four hours.

'Why can't he just call? He must know how upset I am?'

You even call work to say you're feeling under the weather and won't be in this week. How can you face work when you can't even face getting dressed?

Day two and still no word! By the end of day three, you are virtually climbing the wall, going out of your mind. You were determined not to call, but, let's face it, that was never going to last. Your voicemails are gentle enough to begin, but you become increasingly desperate when he, still doesn't respond. His work number has gone dead.

By day four, you are almost begging him to come back practically sobbing down the phone. Still no reply! How could he be so cruel?

For a narcissist, this but is quite easy. He enjoys hearing your messages and knows he has the upper hand.

Visiting his home brings no joy, the lights are out, and there is no car in the driveway. You are going through hell on earth.

And then, five days after the tiff, he calls. He thought five days was enough to teach you a lesson, and you told him he was right by the escalating tone of hysteria in your messages.

The lesson was, of course, never to cross him again. Obviously, he knows you have been round to the house. He has studied the messages, and he knows you have cracked. He tells predictable lies, as only narcissists know how. 'He had to get away, he needed valuable thinking time, he's been depressed recently,' etc., etc.

Of course, yet again you give him the benefit of the doubt even though the evidence against him is overwhelming. He is a total con man and charlatan. Everyone else can see it apart from you, but that said, they don't get to see the inherent qualities in him, only you are privy to.

So you are back together. But unlike last time, don't expect early morning breakfast surprises in bed or a surprise day out. He knows that effort of any kind is no longer required.

From this moment on, you simply become an extension of how he sees himself. You have no other option than to fit in. That is the deal. If you start to operate out with these parameters, the punishment will be the same format but longer.

If you thought this was the extent of the torture, think again. You are about to embark on the final stage of the three-pronged part of a narcissistic relationship. You still have the opportunity to leave with your dignity intact, or you stay and suffer the consequences, becoming a pale shadow of your former self and not uncommon to lose everything you have in the process.

CHAPTER 3

THE DISCARD PHASE.
I'M BORED!

With the combination of your commitment and his control, the first month of living together is as good as it's ever liable to be. Your spirits still lift at the sound of his key in the door, even though the first few seconds can be traumatic till you see what kind of mood he's in.

Up to now, he's been fine, kind, loving, and generous. Though sometimes no words are spoken, it's simply a case of going straight upstairs like two love-struck teenagers squeezing in an illicit affair.

You don't like to think of yourself as being controlled, far from it. It's just that you have finally figured out how to get the best from your partner, and if that involves becoming more accommodating to his needs, then where's the harm in that? All relationships are a give and take, and this is certainly no different. He more than makes up for it by the way he makes you feel, so playing second fiddle as you both settle in together is a price worth paying.

Of course, this is utterly delusional. As one of your dwindling circle of friends pointed this out, you cut her short and have not spoken to her since. He will have advised you to do this as she was only jealous of your happiness.

Narcissists always seem to justify their actions when anyone dares disagree by deluding themselves that the other party must be jealous. Self-awareness is not their strong point. It's always fine for a narcissist to criticize but do unto them as they do you, and you're guaranteed to be on the receiving end of a strong dose of narcissistic rage.

In your deluded world, most things he says now seem to make sense, but unfortunately, his actions never seem to match his words. Your devotion combined with his manipulation is cutting you off from the very people who care for you most. Beginning with your daughter who has gone to live with her father on the pretext of letting you get settled in.

You try not to dwell on the subject, but you were always on good terms with your ex, so she is pleased and in safe hands. The ex has taken over the driving lessons now, as those promises somehow never came to fruition, and it's a subject best dropped.

You often text and speak to her practically every day with the odd tear shared. You remind her that things will work out fine. You just know they will. Being a delusional optimist tends to become part and parcel of living with a narcissist.

Your own house lying empty will be marketed for rent, and, thankfully, as he has friends in this field, he will take care of the admin on your behalf.

'Just leave all this to me, darling. All you have to do is sit back and watch your house appreciate.'

Promises of everything that lies ahead continue to warp your judgment, only clouded by the fact that he has not delivered on any thus far.

Those weekend breaks he guaranteed once a month, and what about that exotic holiday that was top of the list? Since you failed his master test, the extent of entertainment outside of the bedroom so far has been a Saturday night at the cinema followed by a meal in a High Street Pizza chain, on which you went fifty-fifty.

'I get enough fine dining with my job, darling. Sometimes it would just be nice to go out and do the things ordinary people do.'

The night would not be complete without the inevitable criticism.

'Next time, can you show some more cleavage, darling, and slap on some more makeup.'

'Tell you what, why don't I stick a 'For rent' sign around my neck while I'm at it.'

'There you go again, putting yourself down all the time. Listen [narcissists always like to use the word 'listen' at the beginning of a sentence as a form of arbitrary command]. All I'm saying is you look great. I want all those boring guys in the restaurant to know that you're going home to be bedded by me to get them jealous. It's not a lot to ask, is it? You'll be doing it for yourself as much as I. It's all about building up your confidence.'

You reckon?

The male narcissist is a misogynist, holding women in complete contempt. Here you are being tormented, and your compliance with this request [because by now, you know the silent treatment will follow if you don't] is just another example of his control over you. You are merely an object, a source of his narcissistic supply discussed earlier, giving him another 'fix' to his fragile ego. Attention procured from fellow male diners at the next outing will only serve to inflate his delusional feeling of superiority over others, and bear in mind the attention is for his benefit, not yours. Women present will undoubtedly take a different perspective from their temporarily distracted partners looking on with tongues hanging out. Along the lines 'poor woman, if that's how she's made to dress. I'll bet her life must be hell. What a prick'.

His demands, always phrased as though in your favor, continue unabated.

'Why don't you just pack in your job? It's not as if we need the money. We can live comfortably off my salary. Think of all the extra time we can have together and less pressure on you.'

Awwww, this man is all heart.

Well, he does need a cleaner, that's for sure, as describing the place as untidy would be an understatement. As for employing a gardener! Forget it. Guess who will be spending the summer months breaking her back, weeding, and edging?

Narcissists deem such jobs trivial and beneath them. These tasks were designed for inferior people. No matter how desperate their financial position, they would never allow themselves to stoop so low.

Their esteem would be shattered if they were ever spotted with the vacuum out but far outweighing your free labor is the fact that narcissists cannot live alone, ever! They must have someone to do the menial tasks, and they must have an audience for whatever they say or do. Ideally, an appreciative one!

'And do we really need two cars? Everyone gets their shopping delivered online these days, and think of the money you'll save that we can put towards holidays.'

Would that be the exotic holiday he promised or one of the weekend breaks? Saving money, he says, but what about living comfortably off his salary? Things don't appear to be adding up, but then again, nothing seems to be adding up with this guy.

This is all becoming a bit sinister, but you love him even as much as you occasionally despise him. Thankfully in the recess of your psyche, sanity has prevailed, and you tell your first lie.

As a valued employee, your boss allows a six-month unpaid sabbatical, allowing some breathing space for what may, or may not develop. If things go pear-shaped, at least there's something to fall back on. But, for now, you let him believe you have just gone ahead and relinquished your life to his.

Not unsurprisingly, this goes down a treat. You're even taken out for a drink; such is his euphoria. Although once again, he buys the first round, and you the second! You are beginning to learn the rules of the game, albeit in a minor way. But this major victory [in his eyes] lets you keep the car for the time being. On the basis that when the next major repair bill arises, you will gladly kiss your little sweetheart goodbye. Smart move, one you won't regret.

The criticisms continue but with increasing severity.

'You're always doing stupid things. Why can't you just listen to me?'

The loss of income means you have to dip into your savings for the occasional treat. Long days spent cleaning, gardening, washing, and ironing mean little time left for anything else.

You never see the neighbors as, guess what, none of them is his greatest fan. Parking in other people's spaces seems to be one of his most notable characteristics [as always, narcissists don't play by other people's rules but rather make their own up as they go along].

Visitors are nonexistent now, and he's tried to play so many of your friends off against each other. Most have now wisened up and avoid your new home like the plague. Your moods now fluctuate as wildly as his, a fact of which he likes to remind you [especially in public], which does little for your flailing self-esteem.

The bathroom mirror portrays a person who seems strained, and, unfortunately, there is now less money to spend on makeup to disguise the fact. What about the promise of living comfortably off his salary, what happened to that, and every other promise he made? Nothing ever seems to happen. Any money spent on clothes is for him, meaning your own wardrobe gets more dated by the minute.

His social media profile continues to be updated with pictures of him but none of you. Golf days out with friends for which he seems to find the money no problem, but he snaps if you dare mention being taken away for one of those much-promised weekend breaks.

'Do you think money grows on trees?'

What about that well-paid job he claimed to have as an offshore financial consultant, which in reality is probably a euphemism for something a bit dodgy. Your email inbox seems to have become a magnet for dubious companies offering their services for anything from debt consolidation to refinancing long-term loans, adding fuel to the fire that all may not be quite as it seems. [Narcissists are notorious for getting involved in 'dodgy' dealings. They do not think normal rules apply to them, so anything they do is be okay].

Where once there was passion and excitement to compensate for his moods, the evenings he does arrive home [getting later by the day] are now spent watching TV with barely a word spoken.

It is now a no-win situation. You are cut off when you talk as he 'just needs to relax after a tiring day'. If you don't speak, you'll be criticized for lack of affection. What activity was left in the bedroom department has come to a grinding halt. You suspect he may be seeing someone else.

It's nothing major, but you detect, on his detested Saturday grocery run [now your only actual day out], that the front passenger seat has been pulled forward and your five feet seven. Maybe he was just giving a lift to a petite colleague or business partner. Not the first time it's happened, but still, for the sake of keeping the peace, you say nothing. As always!

Funny though, how if you bump into someone at the shops, he gets loving again! His arm will be around your waist, and eye contact reverts to the early days as if you had only just met. Mr. Charming once again is putting on the show as being part of the perfect couple! You walk away wondering if the person who coined the phrase 'familiarity breeds contempt' had ever dated this kind of chameleon.

A letter arrives from your mortgage company, and you are now two months in arrears. What? You thought this was being taken care of by his friends. Your new tenants can prove by bank statement that the agreed rent has been paid, so where is the money going?

Don't worry, he assures you, it is just a temporary cash-flow issue with the funds being used to pay off a loan quickly and thus avoid punitive interest charges. It will all be resolved by the end of the month, and the interest saved can be used for that promised holiday he feels so terrible about. Feeling terrible, feeling guilty, and feeling hurt has become part and parcel of his predictable repertoire.

You bring the bank up to speed, but additional costs have to be met as they were unaware your property was being let. So much for money being saved, and you can guess who will be picking up the tab for the bank charges.

You say nothing, he has got enough on his plate, but this is getting ridiculous.

Not so much a life, more an existence. He's now arriving home later and later, always blaming it on work but with a hint of alcohol hanging in the air.

'Well, of course, I've had a drink. Do you think I actually enjoy these god damn networking events? It's business. How else am I meant to make a living?'

How do you shake off these feelings of being used? It's beginning to grate, especially when he suggests on one of his better days that maybe both houses could be put in joint names. Tax benefits, of course, alongside several other nonsensical reasons which go over your head. But phrased, so it seems he's going out on a limb for you in some way or another. No longer just worrying, this is well and truly scary.

Funny how he always reverts back to being Mr. Charismatic and Casanova in bed each time he ups the ante with financial demands. Whoops, I meant to say requests.

You are so darn close to caving in, but then, your narcissistic partner goes ahead and does what all narcissists do best. They push their luck. They are never satisfied with what they have. Their insatiable appetite proves their undoing but becomes your savior by the same token. Finally, the mist that's been blinding you for the best part of a year is starting to lift.

Yet another weekend of predictable routine and, as always, your food shop as a couple, ostensibly to make sure the food spend is within budget, his budget. Once again, that passenger seat has been pushed forward.

Considering he collected you from the Doctor yesterday afternoon, whoever used the seat only last night. There's something fishy about this, and he has a golf outing that afternoon with clients.

'It's the last one of the season, darling, and if I score with this one, the firm hits the jackpot, and I get a massive bonus, so it's Hawaii here we come.'

You just about manage a smile, but you know he's lying, and it's time you played a detective. Having accepted that just about everything that leaves his mouth is a lie, it should not take Perry Mason to find out what's going on.

Nearly 3 am, the time you calculated he'd be back. The plan of action is in place and ready to be executed. As always, no allowance is made for the possibility you might be asleep. Narcissists must make an entrance, no matter the time of day.

There follows a brief dialogue about how well he played and the great impression he made on his clients. This time around, there's a much more pungent whiff of alcohol, and it's obvious he must have driven home well over the limit. By now, it's clear to you that narcissists have no rule book.

Within minutes he's out for the count.

His mobile-first then car keys!

Surprise, surprise! The passenger seat has been pushed forward again. It's the first thing, perversely, you were hoping to find, and you start thinking of her height. She must be around five, one or two.

A new car freshener is hanging up, but the idiot still managed to leave the cellophane wrapper on the dashboard. He must have done that first thing when he got home as there's been not enough time for it to mask the noticeable odor of perfume apparent the minute you opened the door.

You wonder. Did he book a hotel or just screw her in the car? Probably a hotel in the early days to impress, then just go for the cheaper option, which by now is his trademark. He also enjoys risk.

Narcissists by nature like risk, and shagging her in the supermarket car park half a mile up the road would have been just as big a turn-on as cheating on his partner. The car boot now, and at least he had the sense to include his golf clubs for authenticity, but strangely enough, they are dry as a bone, and his gold shoes are clean. Surprising given that it's been raining all day.

A half-competent philanderer would have had the decency to rub some muck or mown grass onto his equipment but not this guy. Everything about him is half-hearted and amateur. Nice change of clothes to the side of the clubs and the essence of perfume from the shirt you bought for his birthday. Nice touch, as if he's grinding the knife into her back even further.

Now the phone. Sure enough, the moron has yet to delete the last three texts. Two from him and one from her! He goes first.

'Can't get enough of you. Haven't felt this way in years. You're addictive. Xxx.'

'Snap. Missing you already. Don't want to wait as long till next timexxx.'

'Don't worry, will organize during the week. I promise. Luv ya xxx.'

Strangely enough, no convulsions allowing the bile to rise from the pit of your stomach and stain the tarmac. No feeling of desperation, yet, and no sense of emptiness either. The strangest feeling of all is that you still don't want to lose him. It seems he has power over you despite everything he's done to abuse, belittle, and now violate the only thing left, emotional intimacy.

Anyone who has reached this stage in their dealings with a narcissist will testify this is the most tortuous part of all. When the weight of evidence is so overwhelming that any half-decent lawyer would advise, it's not a case worth taking on as there's simply no defense to be had.

Tonight he has gifted you the golden opportunity to walk away with the rest of your life still intact [although somewhat embittered by the experience and financially worse off]. Anyone unfortunate enough to have been there will know exactly how she feels. The love for a narcissist becomes so all-consuming that evidence to the contrary will be ignored. So what's it to be then as this is it. The point of no return and no one else can make that decision for you, although somewhere down the line, someone may have to, as you're in danger of losing your sanity. If you hang around for much longer, you sure as hell will!

⤵

'Anything the matter dear, you seem a bit quiet this morning?'

'No, just a bit of a headache. I think I might have a bit of a cold coming on.'

Two can play at that game, you bastard.

'Are you off somewhere?'

'Yeah, I was thinking I might nip over to the Builders Merchants to see about some replacement fence panels. It's about time I replaced the dud ones at the bottom of the garden.'

Thanks for the concern about me having a cold, bullshit or not. Don't offer to make me a hot drink or nip down to the Chemists. I'll be fine. And since when did grown men visit their local Building Merchants wearing new chino's and brand new Ralph Lauren polo tops?

Guess he fancies some more fun seeing as he's back at the Chapter 1 Idealisation phase with his new woman. He must have texted her from the bathroom. You thought it fell a bit silent after his shower ended. You wonder, are you being tormented, or is this just smugness at a ridiculous level? The answer, a bit of both. But at least you don't need to worry about him thinking he's rumbled so that he'll come hurrying back.

⤻

The first thing to check is the office. You were told in no uncertain terms that it's his place of solitude 'so leave well alone dear'. Everything you need to know will probably be contained within. Strangely enough, it is quite spartan considering the mountains of paperwork he claims he has to process each evening.

Okay, no need to dwell on that one. Just add it to his catalog of bullshit lies. His briefcase has been left open on the desk as obviously putting the fear of death into you about entering is enough to prevent him from locking, and it becomes the little treasure trove you've been waiting for.

Letter from finance company about remortgaging your home and it's been approved. My god, this person really does want to hang her out to dry. You don't need to keep looking as there's probably more dirt to be found on his computer but to what end.

You now have all the evidence you need. Time to make some phone calls, and you suspect the recipient will not resemble the picture already painted.

'Hello, my name is Sarah. Sarah Constance...I am Chris's partner and...'

'Yes, I know who you are,' came the rather abrupt reply. 'I wondered how long it would be before you contacted me...So tell me, Sarah, what stage are you at with Chris now then?'

'Self esteems on the floor, shut me off from my friends and family. Is now playing away and he's determined one way or another to clean me out financially.'

'That sounds just like Chris, alright, so don't expect me to be surprised. Everything you're saying is more or less the same as I offloaded to his first wife. So I take it you've finally caught him cheating? How many has he had?'

'Probably more than I want to know.'

'I take it he told you I was off my head, ran up debts and bled him dry kind of thing?'

'Something like that. You know the script, but I was wondering...'

'Yes'.

'I was wondering if you would like some revenge?'

⤿

Time enough to compose a draft text. Got to get the balance right with this one, but she'll send it in the morning once he's gone to work.

This should do the trick, enough to hook the bait.

'Hi, this is Chris's partner. I know Chris is having an affair with you, and you are probably in a relationship yourself, right? [Calculated guess on Sarah's part] I Am contacting you to help you avoid making the same mistakes I have, and trust me, I have paid a hefty price. If Chris told you the following and has promised you the following, then, if you want to preserve your sanity, I suggest you take my help before it's too late. Now...does any of this ring a bell?

I will be alone after 9 am. I think you might want to call me before it's too late.'

As expected, she calls. This is now cold, calculated revenge, and as far as tomorrow night goes, it will be Chris's turn to think on his feet.

〜

Key in the door once more and some fiddling with the lock, which comes as standard practice for Chris when there's the risk of alcohol being involved! The door gets slammed behind him.

Always an entrance, just letting her know in his usual less than subtle way that she's in for a bad night. His audience awaits in the sitting room, but he's keeping them waiting, and Sarah guesses that one of her guests is about to receive a text message. Boy, is she learning to second guess her narcissistic partner's intentions. It's quite simple once you get the hang of it.

After pouring himself a very large G & T in the Drawing room next door, he clicks the 'send' button, and before you know it, the message has traveled less than six feet through the plasterboard wall. She even manages a half-smile, wondering if he heard the other phone ping less than a second after sending. Her guest responds accordingly.

'Hi, just got home. She's boring me already. I want to be with you. Yu free later? Xxx

'Am free right now. Interested? xxx'

'Yu bet. Give me half an hour to make my excuses.xxx'

'Come see me right now, darling. Am here.xxx'

'Where? xx'

'Next door! xxx'

'What???'

'Yes, lover. Am next door with Sarah! Why don't you join us?xxx'

⌣

This time around, deadly silence. Boy, does Sarah wish she was a fly on the other side of that wall. With no time for Chris to think of plans B or C, he solidifies into a state of frozen panic this time around. Two days ago, he called her his soul mate, and now he's left wondering what on earth the bitch is up to.

No sound for him from next door, not even a squeak. It's kind of become eerily silent all around with both parties wondering who will be first to make their move. With strength in numbers, the girls keep schtum. Narcissists hate the unexpected.

How the hell can you control and come out tops in a situation you know nothing about. Continued silence! Tonight's time is not money. It's a loss of control, and as each second passes, he's losing even more of it. Sarah's played a complete blinder. He takes a straight Gordons' Gin for Dutch courage...then another.

Worst nightmare realized. She would swear that she sees another human being age before her very eyes for the first time in her life. Yet, there, stood before him, stand three women who are not only of similar age but share near-identical experiences with narcissists Chris.

With her mobile held high, Sarah is the first to break the ice.

'What's up, Chris? Are you pleading the fifth amendment? Actually, he wants to scream, such is his searing humiliation, but she kind of knows that by now anyway.'

'No, I'm just wondering what the purpose is of this pathetic little game your playing. I don't know what your intentions are but count me out.'

'Oh come on, Chris [spoken as patronizingly as possible just to rub her handful of salt into his gaping open wound] that was a bit vague, don't you think? You really don't know what to say, do you? So how about I just ask Claire and Elaine here to help me out. Well, of course, you know Claire, considering the pair of you have been seeing rather a lot of each other over the weekend. Here I was thinking you were out there on the golf course while you were holed up somewhere infinitely more snug. I know that Elaine here is itching to tell me everything you did to her, which I suspect, funnily enough, is exactly the same as you've been doing to me. You should really have remembered to delete Claire's messages before jumping on top of me the following morning. Then maybe, just maybe, I would have been stupid enough to keep believing your continual lies. Claire, if you please.'

From a rather sheepish Claire, who must have had her arm twisted so far up her back it nearly snapped, there's a distinctly sheepish response.

'He said that you are lazy Sarah and that you spend all his money. He said...that you are an alcoholic and have mental problems. He wants to leave you, but you keep threatening suicide.' Her voice is cracking all the time, unable to prize her gaze from the floor! She just wants the hell out of here and back to the life she enjoyed, but Chris managed to make her life sound a whole load better with him in the frame. 'He says he feels alive when he's with me...and...and when he sorts everything out, he's...'

'It's okay, Claire. I think we can hazard a guess with the rest, so now it's my turn Chris. Would you mind if I replayed everything you said about Elaine when we first met, and then we can get Elaine to tell us everything you said about your first wife? Now then, Elaine was also an alcoholic and, funnily enough, only ever spent your money. Did you have any idea what he did for a living back then, Elaine? Because I sure as hell don't! Anyway, you also said she was seriously imbalanced with one of the worst family backgrounds you have ever come across, and you said she stopped you from seeing your kids. Isn't it funny, Chris, how much Elaine's story differs from yours? I wonder who I am going to believe in light of what Claire has just said. Now let's talk money, Chris, as you like money, don't you, especially when it comes to getting your hands on other people, then doing a runner just as you did to Elaine and intend doing to me. The same thing, house in joint names, then just keep remortgaging to the hilt to fund your lifestyle. Then, when the going gets tough, you just move on to the next victim and leave the rest of us to pick up the pieces. Does Elaine really need to tell us what you said about your first wife, or can we hazard a guess?'

Feeling guilty that Elaine has merely listened in silence up to now, she allows her to contribute.

'I came up with a script in my head on the way here, but it's pointless really because it's all been said already. So why bother, as the script will always be the same for men like you. It took me years to be rid of you mentally, and Sarah, did you know when you both hitched up, he was still coming round, begging me to take him back, and I even allowed him to stay the odd night. That's even after I allowed him to bleed me dry practically. I guess you just can't live without playing games and doing what you can as long as it brings you attention. I look at you now, and it's not as if I feel nothing because I do. But Chris, what I have is an intense loathing because at heart I feel you are a horrible selfish human being and always will be.'

～

This is truly his worst nightmare. Completely out maneuvered, he never even had an inkling this was coming. This is the trouble with narcissists, and once you cut through the self-perpetuated myth of invincibility, they can be relatively easy to predict.

They may be great at playing games, but in reality, none are that smart. This is why they keep up with the lies, making it seem as if they are cleverer than they actually are. But all the while, the hole they have dug keeps getting deeper and deeper.

Internally his emotions are bordering on volcanic.

You could cut the atmosphere with a knife—time for her guests to make their excuses and head for the door. Claire, in particular, avoiding eye contact at all costs! Hell hath no fury as a narcissist scorned.

Elaine adopts a more pragmatic approach, nothing verbal but unlike Claire's little restraint with eye contact. No need for words when the eyes are perfectly capable of speaking for themselves. Get the timing right, and revenge will always be sweet.

～

Unexpected guests departed, just the pair of you now left alone. Excellent news thinks narcissistic Chris still has time left to work on her. Considering how sensitive narcissists are and taking into account the complete slating he's just had to endure, it's safe to assume she might have been thrown out of the door head first.

But remember, it's a narcissist that takes care of a partner's departure schedule, no one else. So it's time to revisit Chapter one and a charm offensive like no other and as only he knows how. After that, he can kick her into touch once suitably pacified. All she got was a bit too cocky for her own good, stepping out of that little box of hers, but he'll soon have her chained back up inside.

Think about it for a second. What alternative does he have given? There's no way on earth he's going to willingly let her go now that his other bit of skirt has gone running back to the kind of partner Chris could never begin to emulate.

Hate to say it, Sarah, but you are just too valuable for him to lose for the time being. I say again, for the time being. Much easier to handle than that little slut Claire who was becoming a bit too expensive to impress! That's the trouble with arm candy; it's not so cheap anymore, and if she was prepared to stab him in the back now, then what could be in store further down the line?

Risk-taker that he is, could he really afford any more kids? He is teetering on the edge of bankruptcy as it is without needing any more mouths to feed. No, Sarah is generous, tolerant, and forgiving, or from his perspective, a total pushover, but with the additional benefit of being suitably asset rich.

But what about her kindness, generosity of spirit, and capacity to love? Yeah, sure, what about it? Who cares about that stuff when it's the superficial things that carry way more important for your average narcissist.

⌇

But hallelujah, it's been a long time coming, and she's a few kilos heavier, but she's finally out of here. That one remaining bubble of optimism being well & truly burst! The bags are packed, coats on, and as if to highlight the finality of their relationship, within full view, she begins to remove his spare house key from the rest of the bunch. Poor old Chris! He had the bank giving him a hard time this morning, and now he has this to contend with—his one remaining lifeline disappearing before his very eyes.

'What? Were you not even going to say goodbye?'

'I'm not saying goodbye to you, Chris. I'm saying goodbye to the last two wasted years of my life. I'm gone.'

⌇

It looks like the game is well and truly up. This is not the Sarah he knows or, rather, used to know, by the sound of it. The Sarah he came to, well, use. She's just not playing ball anymore, and worse than that, she's outsmarted him every step of the way tonight.

Narcissists just hate to come off second best, so if it's not to be a last push charm offensive, it's looking unlikely a tantrums and theatrics Plan B will work either. What's left then? If the bitch is going to leave, then he will bloody well make sure to destroy those last remnants of self-esteem that gave her the courage to hatch an escape in the first place.

He will crush her so much the cow will be left living like a bloody recluse by the time he's finished, and so the attack begins. Fuelled as much by his own self-loathing as it is by the quarter-liter of gin floating around his system!

'Leave then, but who else is going to have you now? Look at you' grabbing her by the hair and pulling her towards the mirror in the hall. 'On you go, look! Or are you too fucking scared to? See how old you've become and how haggard you are. See the wrinkles as well. Look at them' as he forces her face, so it's now actually pressing against the glass. 'You're old, and you're boring, without a friend in the world. You won't last two minutes without me, and don't expect me to take you back either'.

He's goading you into a fight, but that line of his, remember? 'The person who loses control loses the argument'. It's such a shame he no longer practices what he preaches. He needs retaliation because it brings attention, the life supply of a narcissist. A temporary respite from his greatest fear, that of being alone!

'Why do you think Claire came onto me so strong? It wasn't me. I tried to knock her back, but she just kept coming onto me. You see, I can get another partner just like that [clicking fingers], but who the fuck is going to take you? You're old, you're haggard, and...'

Not goaded. Just the strange feeling for once of finally being the one in control.

'Struggling are we, Chris? You really are struggling because you know it doesn't matter anymore what you say. Do you know why? I don't care. I truly don't care anymore. Everything is an act with you. Your life, your hobbies, fake sports trophies, jobs that never existed, your friends, all these women. You spend your life acting because underneath it all, it is not that you don't like all these women you've bedded behind my back or me. It's not that you don't even like life because the truth is you don't like yourself. I actually think that underneath all this front you put on is an incredibly insecure man with no love for the person that matters most, himself.'

The car headlights appear through the frosted glass window, obviously turning into the driveway as if bang on cue. The sound of a healthy engine being allowed to tick over and waiting! He wonders who the hell else is now going to make an appearance.

'Taxi's here. I'm gone.'

Meticulous planning. Sarah is not for hanging about. She gave him no time tonight. Guess who's had to think on his feet and fallen decidedly short. It's always the way with men like Chris. Do as he says, not as he does. With the front door now open, the first of her three suitcases are on the way out.

'Listen, Sarah, don't do this. Please, come on, you know I didn't mean any of that. It's just me. I'm messed up. Listen, I'm sorry, I'm really sorry. I shouldn't have said any of that. I need help.'

With the second suitcase now heading out, by this time, the taxi driver had appeared on the scene whose sixth sense told him that this job bore all the hallmarks of a domestic, and that was before he'd even opened the door.

'I'll do anything, just stay. Come back in and talk to me, Sarah. Let's work this through. I can change, but I need your help. Please, Sarah, I don't have anyone else.' Take the last as faint praise. He doesn't have anyone else, so you're there to fill the gap now his bit of fluffs has gone back to her partner.

Third and final suitcase heading into the boot, and by now, the poor taxi driver's thinking he wants away from this place quicker than she does. As for the proprietor, this is not his finest hour, and it's desperate stuff.

Not the slightest glimmer of eye contact as she decides to go up front with the driver. It feels safer that way. His pleading face is never more than a couple of centimeters away before the passenger door slams closed, creating its very own shield of defense. How the tables of life turn.

To think she had once been in his shoes but behaving with slightly more dignity. The raised voices have made a few nearby curtains twitch with the odd figure here and there now standing in doorways—free entertainment no doubt but also a touch of schadenfreude for their least favorite neighbor.

Pleading through the front windscreen seems to have had little impact, so there's nothing left for it. It's time to move round the back and spread eagle himself against the boot as if his sixteen stone frame has any clout against the might of a three-liter engine. Raised eyebrows now towards Sarah from the driver! Probably water off a duck's back judging by his size if brute force is required, but there's no need.

'Ignore him, just go. Reverse over the bastard if you have to. I want out of here. Just go.'

CHAPTER 4

TIME TO BE TORTURED

Never one to enjoy awkward silences, tonight, she'll just make an exception. As for the cab driver caught in the crossfire of a dinner-time domestic, it's probably just best to keep schtum. By the time his shift finishes around 2 am, Sarah's tribulation will have been minor compared to the usual Friday night drunken theatrics.

Tonight's depressing situation is only made tolerable by the fact she's now heading back home. Call it a sixth sense, but something told her to just sit on it when word came through a month ago that her tenants had passed up on the opportunity of renewing their six-month lease. By that time, she was playing her cards very close to her chest, another salient little snippet kept hidden, and his philandering had proven her decision to be the right one.

Does living with a liar just make you one? In the end, do all the negative traits of a partner just begin to rub off? One would assume that detecting deceit from an opposing partner would be child's play to a narcissist with these most prolific character traits but surprisingly, no.

Unless being a master of micro-expression, the narcissist will, unfortunately, be as fallible as the rest of us when it comes to pulling blinkers. A good job too, a glance in the downstairs cleaning cupboard might have explained better his concern over Sarah's inability to conceive. Not without trying on his part, of course, as a kid would have been the ideal set of handcuffs, but no such luck. She had to keep her 'pill' stashed somewhere, and the back of the cleaning cupboard was as sneaky a place as any. So, just like Chris, she adhered to the principle of the eleventh commandment—don't get caught.

It's been two extremes in two days! Forty-eight hours ago, she had raised her game, made plans that were executed to military perfection, completely out-thought, and out-smarted a guy who had, unchallenged been running rings around her for the best part of two years.

Out foxed and clueless to cope, his pitiable response has temporarily elevated her spirits, but not for long. The sight of opening the front door to her old place put paid to that. So much for Chris claiming an unpaid friend in lettings management! Just yet more bullshit to add to the catalog of deceit thus far! Now you could call it 'lived in', or you could call it a pig sty, but either way, it's yet another job to take in hand but with the consolation of water-tight insurance cover to fall back on.

Against the wishes of Chris, the master financier of course, 'You don't need insurance, it'll be alright. I've got it all in hand. Look at what else we could do with the money?' Your money, but look at what 'we' could do with it.

Now you just shake your head in disbelief at the perpetual crap that passed between his lips. Home will be sorted and could prove a welcome distraction. You will need a few more distractions over the coming weeks and months as Chris slips up through the gears.

In the meantime, there's only one thing outstanding, and you've missed her like crazy. Hopefully, enough credit is left on the mobile.

'Darling, I am home for good!! Have finally left him. Please, please come home to me. I want to hug you to death xxxxxxx.'

'Mum, are u serious?? At long last, Yippeee. I hated him, mum. Will get dad to bring me now. I missed you sooo much. Want u all 2 myself now. Promise me yur gonna stay for good xxxxxxxxx.'

'I promise. Now get over here ASAP xxxx.'

'Ha ha Am on my way. Luv yu xxxxxxx.'

∽

Twenty minutes later, what appears to be a car stopped outside. Rushing to open the front door, and already welled up at just the thought of Becky sprinting up the path, but the vehicle had already driven off.

Difficult to tell in the winter darkness and already halfway up the street, your eyesight not what it used to be, but was that who you thought it was? Is he just checking? Surely he would have known, but on the other hand, maybe he still expected the tenants to continue making your place worse by the day.

Hate to say it, Sarah, but this is just the beginning. Remember what I keep telling you. They play by their own set of rules so start battening down the hatches.

Handkerchief's at the ready. Becky arrives back just a few minutes thereafter, and that worrying first thought is temporarily cast aside. Tearful hugs aplenty and undeniable reassurance from Sarah that this man is well and truly out of her life.

Even her ex Tom, usually so placid and straight-laced [god what she would do for that kind of man in her life now] behaves completely out of character and loses it, expressing all sorts of concern which will be amplified by the amount of vodka she effortlessly slugs back over the next few hours.

There's no denying this woman has been through the mill. She looks exhausted, not in four straight night shifts in a row exhausted, but mentally caved in. Here's someone that's just come back from a relationship war zone.

Could he be forgiven for feeling just a smidgeon of satisfaction? Possibly, it was Sarah who called time on the twelve-year marriage after all, but no, that's not Tom's style.

Truth was when it happened, and it was not that great a shock, constantly feeling that he'd managed to get away with punching above his weight from day one. She was the girl he met at college, the one all the guys were practically fighting over to sit next to on the bus home, and she'd gone ahead and chosen him.

Not by any means the best looking, but he was nice and easily the most conscientious, wanted to make something of his life, a fact not lost on her mother who was determined at all costs that her daughter would not be making the same mistake she had, that the best looking guys do not always the best husbands make. Was this history doing what it does best, and had Sarah become yet another casualty of believing the grass can occasionally be greener.

∽

Parked up two hundred yards along the street, he stubs out the last from a packet of twenty. Tonight's events have not gone unnoticed. He's seen enough. Now it was time to head back to his very own bomb site after turning the whole house over in the search for hidden clues, including the cleaning cupboard under the stairs and what a good little treasure trove that proved to be.

Pulling away, only one thing on his mind, revenge, and there's some good stuff. Does she not remember in the early days how he liked to take pictures? If only she had spent more time in his office on that famous day.

No doubt helped by the last of the vodka polished off after Tom left, but at least she slept, if you call being out for the count on the settee a healthy night's sleep. She could feel his concern laced with a healthy dose of disappointment, the downward spiral into which she seemed to be sinking.

It had crossed her mind to ask him to stay, a combination of fear and loneliness, but primarily sleeping in the upstairs bed alone, for tonight at least, not her preferred option. Not Tom's way, of course. With her fucked up mind, why make a lousy situation even more disastrous, and why would he want to in the first place.

Unlike Sarah, he's settled, always has been. A happy with his lot, kind of guy. She's the one that always wanted more, always thinking she could do better, and now look where it's got her. Adding insult to injury, all the vodka's gone.

No relationship ending is enjoyable, with one partner usually more affected than the other. To describe the ending of a narcissistic relationship as problematic would be a severe understatement. Bad enough victim Sarah has to rebuild her life from a position as close to the dirt track as possible, but her narcissistic partner Chris, true to the species, does not take rejection lightly.

Again, she did not play by his rules, so she must be held accountable and punished accordingly. By the time the taxi had taken its first corner, the pins were already headed in the direction of Sarah's voodoo doll. Smarter than he gave her credit for, he still knows her weaknesses.

Given her delicate state, it's no coincidence that heartstrings are the first port of call for an ambush. Timing is everything now. The more free time on her plate, the more vulnerable she becomes, and therein lies the most crucial part of recovery—get yourself busy.

Easier said than done, of course, but critical nonetheless. Get out there and reacquaint yourself with long-lost friends, easy in Sarah's case given the amount Chris was so keen to discard. Get the house sorted and throw yourself back into work. Unfortunately, it's commonplace to take the easier distraction route, less effort required, which usually takes the form of drink, drugs, sex, or cigarettes. For Sarah, it's the unhealthier options winning the day.

A lifeline, thankfully, by way of her daughter, Becky. Such was her antipathy towards her mother's ex-partner. She'll be damned if she allows her mum to continue down the destructive path that is self-pity. Her fathers 'everything will work out fine in the end' approach may have merit, but these things don't happen by chance, and why should she have to suffer the consequences on the back of her mum being mucked around yet again. Not that Sarah misses him.

In fact, she barely gives him a mention, just more annoyed with herself for being so oblivious to what everyone else would categorize as bleeding obvious alarm bells.

That old shoot from the hip tells it as if its friend is popping by tomorrow for a catch-up, courtesy of Becky's initiative, and there are umpteen visits to DIY stores planned to get the house back in shape.

All this and the young girl has to squeeze in college along the way. A chip off the old block! A younger Sarah would have had the same approach, and in this instance, she can be considered more fortunate than some women in the same boat. She has company which is crucial if recovery is to gather speed.

Narcissists will do their damnedest to circle the wagons, cutting off those closest at every available opportunity so that when the great day comes and the victim finally leaves, the support network has evaporated once more, leaving them at the Narcissists mercy.

In this isolated mindset, it's always just too easy to put things off, I'll definitely do it tomorrow, but in the meantime, I'll just have one more cigarette or one more drink. This just leads to rumination, a word the author was oblivious to until his association on the wrong end of a narcissistic relationship.

This tendency to overthink, dwelling on matters at an almost forensic level, ultimately leads nowhere and stifles natural physical and mental recovery. Get busy, get active, and get out there socializing. You will be surprised by how quickly predators like this become a distant but unfortunate memory.

For Sarah, unfortunately, this will not happen anytime soon. Now comfortable with her daughter's timetable, having regularly been parked up at the most secluded spot possible, this morning's visit by Chris will be of the extended olive branch, just testing the water variety. Thinking it's her straight-talking friend, the doors get opened with a ready smile that changes to unwelcome shock, a fact that immediately crushes his spirit.

The old charm offensive continues regardless. No mention, heaven forbid at this stage, of the little stash and her deliberate deception. No, no, this is Chris giving it the consummate water under the bridge. Let's forgive, forget but move on as friend's routine. By now, you know what his definition of friends entails. A bit too long on the doorstep for his liking, but she relents, fool that she is, under the proviso she has female company shortly, so it has to be brief.

Harmless as it seems, she has just ignored the No1 rule of post narcissistic relationships. No contact. I repeat, No contact. Did you get that? Once more so the penny drops. No contact. When he turned up at the door five minutes ago, what she should have done was just slam it in his face. The phone rings, you hang up. He sends an email. You delete unopened.

In essence, whatever he does, you ignore. To respond in any way, no matter how negatively, is to acknowledge their existence and, by doing so, signifies in their mind that they are still in with a shout. So the laborious process continues, never being able to break free of their mental clutches.

By now, there will be some key components of your ex-partner's narcissistic behavior you will be more acutely aware of. Devoid of empathy, lack of self-awareness, controlling, manipulative, and greedy, to name but a few! Ask yourself why on earth would you now want to give him the time of day? You do because you are a nice person, not a dumb person but a good person. Who had better start wising up!

You are more worried now that Becky or your friend might turn up at any time than you are about Chris being here. You know only too well they would go ballistic.

But Chris has achieved what he set out to. He's in the door, quite literally, and works his way through the script. This is when the narcissistic hovering begins.

He's so ashamed of his infidelity if only he could turn back the clock; considering counseling, he's not begging exactly, but at this stage, he merely asks you to reconsider. Whatever it takes, he will do to stay in your mind's eye, be it phoning, texts, flowers, or unscheduled visits such as this.

You have it all to come. More concerned with getting rid of him than any form of appeasement, you duly oblige. Yes, you will think about it, but that part took a mere fraction of a second, and fobbing him off for the sake of diplomacy is easier at this stage than a resounding 'No way, Jose'. If only you had shut the door in his face, it would have been much easier. Slamming doors in faces comes later.

Your friend coming along only validates that conclusion without laboring the point too much about her having told you so. More often in life, it's a throwaway line, casual remark, or gesture that can make all the difference between moving on with your life or staying put, and your friend does have this uncanny knack of producing the right line at the right time, which always seems to hit the mark. 'Listen, Sarah, if you're looking for someone to change, trust me, your in for a very long wait'. If there was a modicum of doubt, it disappeared that second.

The game's name is to keep moving on—pity about the loser on the other side of town.

The obsessive texting begins.

'Thanks for seeing me. Just remember the good times. Xxxxx'

You do not respond. Before bedtime, another.

'Sleep well. Lunch sometime? xxxxx'

No response again, and it's already beginning to irritate the shit out of him. If there's one thing narcissists hate, it's being ignored.

◡

The following morning yet another four texts await, but this time you delete them unopened. He is fast becoming rather tedious. Unlike Chris, who seems to have an abundance of free time, you don't, so it's a mid-morning trip to the supermarket to replenish empty cupboards, but guess who's coming towards you in the middle aisle, shoving his trolley from the opposite direction. Just an incredible coincidence or something a bit more sinister? What do you think?

For starters, your trolley is half full, and his contains a single packet of tea bags. Halfway round a supermarket, for god's sake, and all he manages is a solitary bag of tea bags, the cheapo ones as well. Funny how women always notice these things!

No longer looking quite so dapper, unshaven, and anything but color-coordinated. His attempt at feigning surprise is about as lousy as his choice of pretend purchase. Was he always this bad, or is he just getting progressively worse? She hopes the latter. Bad enough, his amateur attempt with the golf clubs, but coincidentally meeting your ex at ten o clock in a particular aisle one of the town's six supermarkets, come on, that's stretching it a bit.

Usual platitudes. For once, you are in control, with shoppers milling around giving you a degree of safety, and you're sure he knows that. Predictable suggestion to grab a quick coffee, you decline. Not even a 'well not today but some other time perhaps' kind of fob off. This was just a straight, put him in his place, no ambiguity whatsoever, don't waste your time, Fuck off.

Nice one, Sarah.

'Why not?'

'Because I don't want to, not with you anyway.'

'You used to say my name.'

'I now just call you other things instead. Now, if you don't mind.'

You move away, and he follows like a petulant child maneuvering his trolley alongside.

'Why won't you talk to me?'

'We both know the answer to that one.'

'Come on, was I that bad?'

'Yes, worse.'

'Sarah, for god's sake. I am not sleeping. I just want you back home.'

Voices now raised and successfully within earshot of the staff member filling up the bread shelves. This has livened up his day. Finally, there is something to discuss other than customers' old complaints about outdated sandwiches in the staff room.

'I'm not coming back. Do you understand? I'm not coming back.'

She moves off, and once again, he follows—persistent bugger, annoying or just desperate. Take your pick or mix and match. Once again, sliding alongside so the wheels practically collide.

'Can we not at least sit down and talk about this. Running around a bloody supermarket is hardly the place.'

'Excuse me,' grabbing the attention of one of the more mature female staff members, and by this time, some tongues are wagging.

'Would you mind asking either a manager or security to deal with this gentleman, who is hell-bent on following me? We used to be in a relationship, but not now, and he won't leave me alone. I don't like it, it's annoying, and I feel threatened. Could you deal with this, please?'

Bloody hell, where did that one come from, Sarah? You being such a shrinking violet as well. Funny how in adversity, some people just seem to rise to the occasion. Hardly any use for his street cred, and you never know, all it takes is just one neighbor to be in the wrong place at the wrong time, and he can kiss any remnant of respectability goodbye.

He shuffles away with eyes fixed firmly ahead, conscious that there's a little room in this building somewhere with a bank of monitors, and he's being tracked as he passes through each one. The date, the time, and the place. It's all evidence, Chris. Fancy her having the audacity to stand up to him in a public place. Yet another under estimation. Fucking bitch.

This has been a productive morning. Standing up to a bully takes guts, but then again, there's that old cliché about them being insecure as hell underneath. He'll lick his wounds, go away and bed the next lonely forty-five-year-old who's looking for some spice in her life.

Good luck to him, good luck to them, not your problem anymore, but at least you're aware of the tactic. No matter how lousy it was, that by fair means or foul play, usually the second, the narcissist tries his damndest to stay in your head.

A year ago, confrontations like these had you heading for the off-license but not now, just too many damned things going on in your life. Beginning this afternoon with a trip to the hairdressers and some retail therapy. If you're going to be seeing your old boss again, it always helps to look the part.

Is this another one of those passenger seat moments? Returning home, something's not right. You feel it. You know it. Has that bastard been in here? How could he? You took the spare key from his bunch on the hall table when you left. That must have pissed him off.

The back doors are okay, and the windows are fine. No carpet marks from the rain outside, and the clown would never have been smart enough to remove his shoes in the first place. Upstairs is fine but the bedroom door, did you close it that far?

Everyone has their little quirks, which a partner will soon pick up on, and Chris always seemed to leave doors barely ajar. Said it was to keep the heat in. Fuck, this guy has got you nearly as paranoid as him. Hurry up and get changed.

For your part, you might have played your own little game of subterfuge, with keeping a secret in the downstairs cupboard but come on, your forgetting he also had his little safety deposit boxes scattered around back home. Is the toolbox at the back of his garage the kind of place you would likely go looking for your spare house keys?

You were clocked coming out of the Hairdressers, and he is pretty good at this to give him his due. Not even a clue you were being followed from home, yet traffic was pretty sparse. Quickly spotted if in the wrong lane or creeping forward just a shade too far, that's an experience for you, but let's remember he does have form in that dept. Elaine could have told you so.

Half an hour extra in her company on the night of the long knives would have let you know what to expect, especially the importance of going no contact, once the decision has been made. I point which I reiterate once again. In fact, I intend to repeat until you are sick to the back teeth of hearing it.

Unfortunately, having been deprived of this crucial piece of information, Sarah is now only moments away from the realization of every woman's worst nightmare that she is now being stalked.

He keeps a steady pace: thirty yards minimum, fifty maximum distance. Always keeping an eye on the nearest bus shelter or shop doorway to dive for cover. So far, so good. Easy to see what the bitch is up to, plain as can be. She's been cheating on me all along. Fucking Hairdressers and now in and out of clothes shops. Why else would she bother? She never did that for me.

Yes, Chris, because you never allowed her, that's why, but in this delusional frame of mind, he takes some bog-standard female behavior and contorts it into something designed to suit his irrational thinking, that there's now another man in her life.

All stalkers, whether narcissistic or not, have usually been involved in intimate relationships and simply refuse to accept when the relationship is over. Their control over their partner during the relationship is over, and their worst fear is realized.

Without this control, they lose all feelings of self-worth and lose their identity as being part of a couple was the central building block of this identity in the first place. They, therefore, begin stalking, trying to regain their partner and the power that existed alongside it. It is this total dependence on having a partner for identity that makes a stalker so dangerous.

They will go to any lengths, and if Chris cannot win Sarah back, his life, in his eyes, is truly not worth living. Starting from the initial invitation to coffee, which she refused, things have now escalated to believing his greatest fear and paranoia descends.

He convinces himself that Sarah has met another man and will leave him. In his mind, he has convinced himself of that conclusion, and if he can't have her, then no one else will.

Yet another High St chain to visit,

Of course, Chris interprets this as an over-eagerness to look the part for the new man in her life. This time it's a more suitable selection with which to browse. By loitering at the front door, he can quite easily come across as just another bored husband being made to suffer while the other half fritters away his hard-earned cash better used to pay the bills.

No danger of the cover being blown as a stalker on the prowl. Buying a newspaper from the vendor by the door adds another bit of authenticity to the charade.

Occasional glances but then, what the fuck, he's lost her. She could be in one of the changing rooms, of course. Highly likely, but dear oh dear, big mistake.

Having left by a side door, she comes back up the short alleyway to bring her back onto the main street, and guess who she sees, craning his neck for the optimum view to the back of the store.

None other than Mr 'Always falls at the last hurdle' Chris. This time incandescent, she's pulling no punches. An attack from behind will always leave your opponent vulnerable, and guess who's now having to think on their feet.

'What do you think you're playing at? Why are you following me?'

'Ehh...I was just passing. I just thought I saw you go in here.'

'Don't lie, you're following me. You've been following me all day, and I know you've been driving past the house. What the fuck do you think you're playing at? I'm sick of it.'

'No, I'm not. I just saw you and thought we could talk.'

'I don't want to talk to you. I don't want to see you ever again. Do you understand? Get it into that thick skull of yours. We are finished. Do you understand? We are finished.'

'Why did you have to cheat on me? I always knew you were seeing someone else...?'

'What? Don't start all this bullshit all over again. I'm not playing your pathetic little mind games anymore. Just fuck off and leave me alone.'

'I can't. We just need to talk. Why don't we sit down and work this out? I'm only trying to be reasonable.'

'You, reasonable? Give me a fucking break. You're a disaster. You hear me a disaster. Now...'

'Sarah.'

Her voice is breaking, and tears are beginning to stream. She barely manages her final tirade of abuse.

'Just fuck off, will you. Leave me alone and fuck off.'

⤳

So much for no Contact! How many times have I mentioned this, and there you go being drawn into a street fight where, quite clearly, there will only ever be one winner. You may have one the verbal battle, but he's miles ahead with the mind games. Who's the sore loser now?

An entire day all but ruined you scurry off in search of the nearest large vodka followed by a visit to the same said supermarket the nonsense all kicked off with this morning. The correct thing to do would have been to ignore and walk past as if invisible completely. Most solutions are never that complicated. Knowing what to do, though, is one thing. Having the composure or stomach to put the solution into practice, quite another.

⤳

One item is only required, and it's not cheapo tea bags. You were tempted this morning but managed to refrain. Now it's more a case of absolute necessity. Those liter bottles at 8.99 are now just too good to turn down. Pity the offers are restricted to three only. You buy your maximum allowance.

As for Chris, driving home, he is composed on the outside but internally still really pissed that he got caught. That side door, fuck, he should have checked. That's the way with narcissists.

Complacency is always the greater threat than the enemy itself. Okay, so he got caught, but she might still come back. It's happened before, but in this case, the bitch has gone ahead and found another man.

Another man screwing his partner, now for a narcissist, is the ultimate knife in the back. With Elaine, it was much easier. Pretty, but only in a moderate way, flat chested with no natural curves, why would anyone else bother. But this one's different. She's attractive and still has it.

Yeah, sure, the backsides got bigger, but you could still work that off her given half a chance. You just have to make sure this new guy doesn't get a look in. Do whatever it takes to put him off. Scaring him away would be even better. Opening the front door to yet another unpaid local authority tax reminder, he kicks it aside and heads straight upstairs to the sanctity of his office.

As always, the door is left slightly ajar. This is now his war room. Stalking affairs coordinated from within this bombsite that masquerades as a financial consultant's office. The juicy stuff, the photographs are in the bottom drawer of the computer desk. Every office visit involves a drawer check. These pictures represent his ultimate bargaining chip, but there's still phase two to initiate. Time to send another text.

'I know you are angry and confused, but things will work out fine, believe me xxxx.'

Driving home, paranoia descends. Is she being followed? 'What if he's not in his BMW?' [Actually, he's not, the finance company repossessed] 'What if he's already at home waiting? Is he now watching Becky, Christ Becky, she hasn't texted you today. If that bastard lays so much of a finger on her, you swear to god you'll kill him.

Stopping for petrol 'Who's coming in from behind? Has he got other people in on the act? The van driver filling up opposite seems to be watching you? That car had pulled up at the pump tight behind yours when there were lots of other spaces free. Another single bloke who gives a two-second glance! Everyone seems to be watching you. You want to get out of here, and you want to hide.'

Having paid, she pretends to fumble with her handbag, waiting for the van and car to pull away first. The van driver glances over once more. Actually, he quite fancied her, but of course, she sees it completely out of context. Not the done thing, and it has to be quick.

Once the cashier moves out of sight, the vodka comes out of the carrier bag. As good as any park bench alcoholic, she manages a couple of good slugs, and by god, it hits the mark. $8.99 own label can be as good as any brand name when needs must. This is on top of the two doubles consumed an hour ago. Lady luck better be on her side for the twenty-minute drive home.

Chris has done rather well. Transforming her to a nervous, neurotic wreck in the space of fewer than eight hours takes some doing. Throw in a ten-minute house intrusion [yes, he did take his shoes off], and you have all the hallmarks of a successful day in the life of a stalker.

Tempted to scare the shit out of her by leaving a packet of her contraceptive pills in the top drawer of the bedside table, he refrained. Good job too, a stunt like that could have been the tipping point that sent her to the nearest flyover with a suicide note. All he has to do at the computer now is come up with a half-decent stage name, enter a few basic details, is she a 34b or a 34c, think of a decent profile, and upload one or two decent pics.

Heh presto, the job is done. It took all of fifteen minutes, and now Sarah, without your realizing, you have just joined one of the black economy's more lucrative professions. If you are paranoid when the postman knocks on the door, you haven't seen anything yet.

⸽

Every day is now a challenge. She is a recluse in her own home, unable to muster the courage to step outside to the full view of those prying eyes. Constantly checking the back door then rechecking it's locked.

Peering out of the bedroom side bay window to look for any cars parked that she doesn't quite recognize and watching dog walkers slowing down as they pass by to pick up the dog dirt. Who are his accomplices? How many are there? The bed you shared now seems dirty, violated. It appears that the person you had right there and in love with has returned in a different guise to haunt you.

Encouraged by Becky and Tom to contact the Police, you refuse, for the time being anyway. Maybe he'll just go away once he finds somebody else. No one else knows, and the phone has yet to be used to contact anyone, apart from when Becky calls to touch base. You dare not use it in case someone is listening in. One of the liter bottles is now finished, and the second is a third of the way down.

That's no sleep in two days, quite literally, and it's showing. Becky's called up your old boss to say your bed ridden with a chest infection. But how long can you play that card? Sooner or later, someone else may come along and fill your shoes. You may have been popular, but you're certainly not indispensable.

From Becky leaving at ten past eight for the bus, it's a progressive countdown till she calls in at bang on 11:17 am, the time agreed between the pair of you that it's safe to answer.

Already there have been five withheld numbers trying unsuccessfully to get through. If Tom can escape from work, he makes it for ten to one. Of course, he has to be there at that time, so you're sure who it is. Even leaving the security of the living room once Becky has left proves difficult enough.

∽

Bang on time, it's ten o clock and a friendly rat tat tat on the front door. Talk about a shiver down your spine. Has he come to try and talk her round or place his hands firmly around her throat? You ignore. Another polite but marginally louder knock, and no, it's not Chris, this guy looks nothing like him.

Actually, his name is Simon, age 55, works as a Civil Engineer, married with four kids, his wife works as a Primary Teacher, and they've been together twenty-two years. He allows himself the odd indulgence now and again, seeing as the mortgage is paid off and school fees are over.

Sarah's new alter ego 'Shanisse' sounded just about right, and she's undoubtedly handy, he only lives three miles up the road in one of the more sought-after areas, and if she's any good, he might start a new jogging route with his twice-weekly runs.

'Come on, answer the door, for god's sake.' Punters hate to be left standing on doorsteps, self-consciousness takes over, and doubt creeps in. 'Is this really such a good idea?' One hundred and fifty quid for an hour.

What else could you use that money for instead? He doesn't hang about. This smells dodgy. If the door never opens within two minutes, then you know something's not right. It looked too good a street to have a whore house slap bang right in the middle in the first place! Win some, lose some.

She's spied him through the net curtain. Tall, well built, smartly dressed, and carrying a briefcase which he always used as a prop. Maybe he was selling something or, more likely, another dodgy financial associate of Chris. That idiot would do anything to get his greedy little mitts on her house.

Becky checks in at 11.17 am. Bit of a scare, probably nothing to be alarmed about given you're over-sensitivity, but you're okay.

Same again, this time bang on twelve o clock. Rat tat tat, less friendly, slightly more officious knock on the door this time. Bang on the hour, it's as if these guys have appointments. Well spotted. Your brain's halfway there. Who is it now?

Same guy, Chris, different guy? Something's going on. No cold callers since you moved back, and now, two in the space of as many hours, the day after Chris morphed from ex-partner to stalker.

Yet another officious knock of the 'I know you're in, so don't think I'm going away' variety. It can't be Chris. He is more likely to plead through the letter box, although you're now sure the bastard has a spare set of keys anyway, so why make life difficult for himself and attract the neighbors.

You seize the initiative. Dutch courage, more assisted by the rapidly depleting supply of vodka than by the strength of character.

Tentatively opening the front door, the view from the opposing side is most definitely not as per the booking schedule. So much for the negligee, heels, and hair tied up as requested.

Not exactly asking the earth when it's a hundred quid for the half-hour. Yet another man in his fifties! Smartly dressed but more High St than tailored, and distinctly ill at ease! If she only knew why she would no doubt empathize. A look of suspicion on her face and disappointment on his.

'Have I got the right address, love? Twenty-two Northwood Rd?'

'Yes, you have. What do you want...I mean, what can I do for you?'

Christ, look at her. Tracksuit bottoms, t-shirt, and hair that looks like it's been dragged through a hedge. Not sure he wants to be here anymore, but beggars can hardly be choosers, and he isn't having much luck on the internet these days. She could probably scrub up better if she wanted to, and for a hundred quid, she should.

'Are you the girl that calls herself Shanisse?'

'I beg your pardon?'

'Shanisse, love. I've got a booking for half an hour with Shanisse. Are you Shanisse, or is it another girl?'

'What? [Penny dropping] Are you saying what I think you're saying?'

'Well, it was a booking for twelve o clock. You accepted my request.'

⤿

Slam the door time or think on your feet instead. Make it the latter, the better of the two options, not helped by the alcohol, but you try your best.

'Can you help me here? Is this a wind-up?'

'So you're not an escort?'

'No, of course, I'm not. I'm not fucking Shanisse, nor is there anyone else in the house called Shanisse. So you came here thinking I was a prostitute? Who told you to come here? Who gave you my address?'

'I got it on the website, the Adult Angels website.'

'Adult Angels? What, and I am on Adult Angels. How am I...I don't understand?'

'Have a look for yourself, love. It's all there. I guess I better be going.'

'I guess you better had.'

⤸

Somethings happened. Too much dialogue on the doorstep, for one. It helps that he no longer has the BMW, and being parked behind one of the neighbors affords some nice camouflage just when he needs it most. No shouting, no hysterics, and no doors slammed.

It could well be the punter's gone ahead and spilled the beans. Smart phone from jacket pocket and profile deleted in the time it takes to say 'On your knees sweetie.' Try proving that one, Sarah.

Bad news, though, Chris. You're now not the only one that's being watched.

⤸

Unable to recover, his behavior becomes progressively more alarming. Narcissists hate to be beaten, which is why they seem to up the ante with their unsavory behavior when the present tactic appears to be flagging.

A smear campaign is about as low as it's possible to sink, but it will have been instigated long before Sarah called time on his extracurricular shenanigans. It's a kind of safety net in the early days so that when the shit finally does hit the fan, and he's caught red-handed, the blame can easily be attributed to her mental instability or tendency to overreact.

Those friends deemed suggestible enough to fall for the narcissistic charm will have been primed by being drip-fed sufficient information about just how hard living with Sarah can be and the sacrifices made to keep the relationship alive. Narcissists are very adept at playing the woe is me victim card.

As she only ever had one friend daft enough to give him the benefit of the doubt, his options are limited with smearing, so anyone and everyone prepared to listen becomes the order of the day. In this instance, dishing out flyers to neighbors about the whore house down the road is about as good as any, on the basis that mud sticks.

Sometimes it does, but in extremis, and when highly unlikely, it is usually laughed off. He shouldn't have assumed that everyone believes what they read.

Thank god for Tom arriving at the allotted time, always Mr dependable but, crucially, Mr. Reasonable. His role for the first hour is to listen because describing Sarah as incandescent would be an understatement. No, she will not be allowed to drive over to Chris's house with a meat cleaver. At least someone understands the principle of no contact.

Of course, this is what Chris wanted in the first place. Any method of action for a narcissist is worth pursuing if the result brings attention. In this instance, turning up at his doorstep, half cut, for a confrontation would only add to the persona of the deranged ex-partner he is now so desperately trying to paint.

Tom is well built and in the building trade, can easily fend for himself, and dissuade others from hanging around at the front door should any more frustrated fifty-year-olds come calling. He will also be stopping over now for peace of mind. The name of the game, hard as it seems, is to get back on track. She may have been happier if the past two years had been spent stuffing her face with chocolates and listening to

Leonard Cohen CDs, but she is where she is and just has to deal with it.

Don't be fooled that narcissists don't know that you want to move on, but it's their role to try and throw you off course again and again and again. Unless you move on, you will always be two steps forward and four steps back. Just get back on the horse and keep going.

↩

Inactivity only breeds isolation, which further fuels dependency. The vodka has been coming in. Setbacks further a retreat into seclusion, and so begins a vicious circle of alcohol, filling a void. You have a social network on which other victims are not so fortunate and capitalized. Of course, there will be setbacks, and these will continue in the short term, but nothing lasts forever.

The irony is that for the time being, you are the only support mechanism in place for the social malcontent Chris. His increasingly futile tactics are designed to reestablish some form of contact to fill his desperate void from which you are, at the moment, his only means of escape.

You have to make him realize his efforts are ultimately pointless. You are on the right track. Just keep going and get back to work as soon as possible. Isolation leads nowhere.

↩

'Sarah, we need you back here pronto. We're desperately understaffed, and everyone's complaining about the workload.'

Refreshing in today's climate, your old boss is still such a man of his word, but why do you get this niggling feeling that a rabbit is waiting to be pulled out of the hat. A notepad he keeps referring to, which is out of character for him. It's like he has something to say but can't quite bring himself to say it.

He's straight as a dye but lousy at the emotional stuff. He's beginning to shift awkwardly in his seat, and that thing he does with his hand when under pressure, brushing his hair back with his hand.

Something's about to give. He's just so damn uncomfortable now that you find it quite funny, so you take the lead. The build-up's much more amusing than the content, though.

'Well, what is it your avoiding telling me? I know something's troubling you. I know what you're like with stuff like this. Trust me, after the past few years I've had, I can handle it.'

'Can you? I hate this stuff, Sarah, but Human Resources always put this shit onto me. All this about chain of command and all that.'

'So, what is it?'

Preferring to look at his notes instead of her, he takes a deep breath before he finally manages to blurt out a response.

'Human Resources have received correspondence recently. I was going just to lie and tell them I'd spoken to you about it anyway as I know it's all crap but...'

'Will you just get to the point, Bill?'

'Right, some fucker has told them you have a serious drink problem and that you've been having an affair with. I won't mention who, her husband, and that he's been trying to call it off, but you won't take no for an answer. They're worried that if she finds out, the shit hits the fan, and where does that leave the atmosphere in the office? As your contract had expired by mutual consent, there's no obligation to take you back, so why make trouble for ourselves, notwithstanding, of course, your impeccable record to date. Why would the fuckers want to have this kind of sensitive discussion when they can pass the buck onto me and cover their asses? Like I said, I was going to lie anyway, fuck me, it's been over two years since we've seen you, Sarah, and things happen, but I know you well enough to tell when some idiots got a grudge. That's exactly what I told them. Some idiots got a grudge, so throw the bloody letter in the bin, but you know what it's like nowadays. Everything has to be looked at and investigated. So that's it, Sarah, and I now feel hellish for just having told you this. Trust me, I want you back, that why I said it, but the buggers have said it has to be at best a rolling six-month contract, well, for the time being, that is. I'll soon have it changed. Well, go on, say something?'

'Why am I not surprised? Is that good enough for you?'

'I take it you've had an eventful time of late?'

'You could say that. If you call being controlled, manipulated, cheated on, fleeced, stalked, and being accused of being a whore and now a husband snatcher eventful? Well, kind of' yes. In a nutshell, Bill, my ex, is out to destroy me.'

'Is this the same guy we all thought was the bee's knees? He seemed a top bloke, or is it, someone, since?'

'No, same one. That very same guy who had everyone fooled, especially me. It's been a disaster of epic proportions, and now he's trying to get to me through work. Where does it all end?'

'You could contact the Police?'

'And where will that end up? Try proving anything. He's such a slimy bastard he would probably fool them too. Mr nice guy, butter wouldn't melt. Paint me as a deranged middle-aged woman who's lost the plot. He does it to everyone he meets. I truly hate this man, and he's now beginning to really get to me. I'm at my wit's end, cant sleep, and yes, I've been drinking but only since I left. It could have been anything if it hadn't been alcohol, but in this case, he guessed right.'

'But you're well enough to come back?'

'I want to come back more than anything. In fact, I need to come back for the money as well as saving my sanity.'

'In which case, Sarah, the sooner, the better. How about tomorrow?'

'And what about Human Resources?'

'Consider the matter closed.'

⟿

Chris is watching her coming out of the building, but it's hard to gauge her mood. She seems sullen, which is a good sign, but if this hasn't worked, there's only one thing left for it, the powder keg back home in the bottom drawer. That should put paid to any boyfriends, once and for all.

The tricky bit is now finding the time. Another bit of stuff on the go, no real prospects, but he'll take what he can get at the moment, and of course, she's another nice girl. Once Sarah's back, this new one can fuck off back to the dating site and try her luck all over again.

Clocking her the following Saturday night, leaving the house to meet her close friend for a drink only fuels his concern that she's meeting the new boyfriend. But his pursuer is beginning to realize this guy is never going to leave Sarah alone unless he takes direct action...'

A group of women out on a Saturday night, who needs men? But of course, guess what's the favorite topic of conversation, especially when one of the group seems keener than most for some advice. A change for Sarah to be the listening ear for once.

The poor woman met this great guy online who ticks all the right boxes, but 'Uh-Oh' Sarah's saying to herself as he seems to blow hot and cold. One minute mad keen, then he's off, and she doesn't hear from him for days on end. Predictable responses from most of the women, but she prefers to keep listening.

'I swear to god if he was here, you would like him, but I just don't know.'

Sarah's heard enough, and it's time for some questions.

'In the early days, did he make you feel alive? Give the impression that finally here was the one you've been waiting for all your life. A connection like no other?'

'Well, yes, that's exactly it. Cant put my finger quite on it, but we just connected in a way I've never felt before.'

'And did he spoil you endlessly with promises of what's yet to come?'

'Exactly, how do you know all this?'

Sarah's bullshit detecting friend affords herself a wry smile at the killer punch line waiting in the wings'

'Just one more, has he been married before?'

'Yes, he's very open about this. He's told me everything about his past. She sounds like a real nut job. Think that's what made him so wary.'

'Well, take it from me. Lick your wounds and head for the hills. I can give you the script if you want, but I've been there before, and I am still paying a hefty price.'

'What, from just that? how can you tell?'

'Because I can, trust me, that's enough.'

Her friend interjects. 'Now you know why I brought you along.'

'And I don't mind, honestly. I'll give you my number, my new number I hasten to add as I've had to change my old ones because the bastard was such a pest. Call me anytime, but please, please, please drop this guy like a hot potato. Don't end up like me. The word torture doesn't come into it.'

'But how could someone like you be taken in. You're attractive, confident, and intelligent. How could any guy pull the wool over your eyes?

'Because they are cunning, deceitful, manipulative bastards, that's why, and most women will be suckers at some point in their lives. I can already tell you're a lovely girl. That's why you were chosen.'

'Chosen?'

'Yes chosen, selected, call it what you like. Trust me on this. Get out while you can. Like Jane once said to me. I'm telling you not what you want to hear but need to know'.

A successful night! Hopefully, one life saved from another menace out there plying their trade.

∽

The momentum continues. Work during the week, not a drop of alcohol touched outside of socializing with girls. The odd night at the pictures with Becky and, as a thank you to Tom, cooking dinner this coming Saturday night.

The first time the three of them will have sat down together since Becky was starting Secondary. No longer a kid, on Saturday, she officially becomes an adult when Tom takes her to collect her first car. Definitely, something to celebrate at the weekend.

Becky is over the moon, brand new, and I mean brand new. How good is Dad to me? Nifty little sports car bought on one of those three years never deals. She's made every excuse possible to drive Mum here, there, and everywhere.

She gives it another polish, as if it was needed, and peers out the front window every fifteen minutes to check it's safe and sound. She's high as a kite and even more so as Dad's coming round again at eight o clock for his tea. Home-made Lancashire Hot Pot and Sticky Toffee pudding.

Just like the old days, the three of them together as a family. Sarah's even spent the day cleaning, and it's not gone unnoticed by her daughter how much she's looking forward to him coming back round.

He might be a comfort blanket now, but a very loving, warm one at that. Just a pity someone's determined to throw a spanner in the works. Tom's always on time, but he'll be early for a change just to be on the safe side. Funny how he just has this feeling.

Sports car parked outside, he fucking knew it. The bitch now has him in her bed, and it's his bed. Fucking bedroom lights on as well, don't tell me he's undressing her already. Parking up, he just needs a minute to compose himself. Get the envelope out, and hopefully, the boyfriend will be the first to open the door.

He won't hang around when he sees the photographs, and he'll be off in a shot. See her for what she really is. Always parked at the blind spot just out of view, it's time to roll without paying too much attention to the white transit parked thirty yards in front or the heavily built man just stepping out and looking like he's collecting some tools.

By the time he smells a rat, it's already too late, Tom's coming fast, and his features are already showing their intent. A short punch but driven with ferocity straight into the pit of the stomach. Never saw it coming, no time to breathe in to cushion the blow.

Immediately winded, he's bent double with one of his arms now brought up behind his back. He's steered around the other side of the van against the railings and out of sight. Those early years as a student bouncer have served him well. Still struggling to breathe, Chris is now pinned against the side of the van with a builder's solid hand clamped firmly around his throat.

'Now what do we have here? More dirt to use against a woman who can't defend herself? Well, you won't be wanting these any longer, will you? You know what, matey, I despise guys like you. You come along playing your little games, promising women the earth, then come back to haunt them when they can't put up with your shit anymore. You don't just make their lives a misery, and you make decent blokes lives a misery as well when it's left to us to pick up the pieces.'

Builder's hand now gripped even tighter.

'So help me, god, if I even smell you within five miles of Sarah, I'll fucking finish you off. Do you understand?

Another squeeze with the airwave practically blocked, he nods agreement.

'The first one was for Sarah, and now this one's from me.' Another blow lands straight on target, and he's now pissed himself into the bargain.

〜

The Hot Pot went down a treat, and the Toffee pudding was to die for. So Becky, ever the diplomat, now makes her excuses and retreats upstairs to milk social media for all its worth, knowing full well Mum and Dad might, just might, be seeing more of each other.

'I meant to ask you when you came in tonight did you hear some shouting?'

'What, oh that. Think it was just a couple of drunks fooling around.'

'Tom, are you sure that's all it was?'

'Quite sure, Sarah. When have I ever lied to you?'

It's been a long time coming, but the Sarah smile of old has finally come back.

∽

Across town, another middle-aged woman begins to doubt her choice of a new partner.

CHAPTER 5

NARCISSISTS AND ATTENTION

Do I like attention?

Of course, I do, but everything is in moderation and preferably in a positive way. I don't do the negative stuff very well at all. Too much attention and I begin to think 'Yes ok, that's enough thank you, now pack it in'. Too little, or none at all, and I can't say that it bothers me that much. The odd compliment for a job well done or that old favorite 'Heh, you're looking well' can usually suffice. But, of course, this is my subjective opinion.

I accept that there's always going to be a disparity between the Actual and Preferred way we see ourselves, but on the scale of attention-seeking behavior, I allow myself a score of maybe a two or three out of ten. I leave it to friends or colleagues to decide whether or not I live in the real world. 'He said what? Two or three out of ten!! Are you kidding me?'

Could I ever qualify for entry as even a 'D' lister in today's celebrity-driven culture? Nope, never in a zillion years. But why would I want to?

To put yourself forward to appear in some banal reality television show performing tasks beneath that of a trained monkey for the sake of being in the public limelight would be enough to drive me nuts [excuse the other monkey pun], notwithstanding the five-figure cheque that usually works as a sweetener.

Would I do it if I were even that skint? I like to think not, but the subject has been the source of differences in opinion. Those that disagree don't know me well enough. Hell, that's my story, and I am sticking to it! Allowing for perilous finances, I'll give my thoughts on why some people, predominantly narcissistic, feel the need to engage in this kind of nonsensical behavior. This will likely be of the teaching you to suck eggs variety.

Was I different in my younger days? You better believe it, but I like to think this was more vanity than narcissism. In my twenties, I was in the Navy, an officer no less. Having a uniform with a couple of rings on the shoulder gave me, finally, a bit of kudos.

Back then, I thought I scrubbed up rather well. I may have looked in the cabin mirror the odd hundred times or more than was necessary. Still, I enjoyed looking the part, especially when it came to any admiring glances I may have garnered from ladies onboard for the odd cocktail party.

Ahh, those were the days and how times have changed. Was my behavior back then narcissistic or just the vanity of early adulthood, a time when most of us will be enjoying our time in the sun, safe in the knowledge that grey hairs are only just around the corner.

For ships, sometimes holding two to three hundred men, well, that's a lot of male testosterone flying around in a contained environment. Certainly, there were always those who did what they could to stand out from the crowd, especially when it came to social events. This was the 80's remember when narcissism was nowhere near as prevalent as it is today. But, without realizing it at the time, the summer of 1986 and an Engineer called Maurice were my introduction to the subject in general and attention-seeking in particular.

Maurice was a good-looking guy back then, probably in his early thirties, blessed with a good physique and ready smile. Great teeth, as I recall. The type could just effortlessly walk into the officer's mess, and he would be holding court within minutes.

I was fixated, just standing in the corner as I usually did, watching others gravitate towards him. Awarding myself a two or three out of ten in attention-seeking, I was hardly destined to set the world on fire in the personality stakes.

The term shrinking violet never did me justice. I had never got round to speaking to the guy, so all I could do was observe from the sidelines, but no doubt I was slightly in awe of him. I just had to wait my turn before I was granted an audience, but somehow I knew I'd already been clocked.

What took the shine off, when the moment eventually came, was that Maurice liked to be known as 'Maureeece' with an emphasis on the 'eeece'. You actually had to call him 'Maureeece' to be awarded friendship.

Nowadays, that would be one hell of a narcissistic indicator. Still, I duly obliged, never feeling entirely comfortable having to suck up. Still, needs must when you are a new boy on a vast ship, so I made my introductions, even practicing the 'eeece' several times in my cabin to get the intonation just right. Get it wrong, and his eyes cut you in two. Even the Captain called him 'Maureeece.' Christ, how good is this guy, I thought, when even the big chief is dancing to his tune?

It seems glaringly obvious now, but I should have known, hell, we all should have known, how the name reinvention came about. The Steve Miller band's hit 'The Joker' had reappeared in the charts in the early '80s. Three verses in, and you find the source of his inspiration.

'Some people call me the space cowboy, yeah

some call me the gangster of love

some people call me maureeeeece.'

༄

Listen for yourself, and believe me, the intonation had to be just right or else.

༄

My first taste of a Naval cocktail party, and there we all are in our dicky Bow's, waist-length white jacket and cummerbunds, jockeying for position with whatever few female ex-pats may have been in attendance.

It was usually a case of 80:20, so your opening line had better be good, or it was goodnight Vienna. What chance did a shrinking violet have, irrespective of how well he thought he scrubbed up?

So I was just happy. If happy is the right word, resigned may have been a better way of putting it, to just stand on the sidelines and observe. Needless to say, 'Maureeeece' was always right in the thick of it by the time it became a full house, but before you could say 'Can I have another Pimms please' he was gone, to the loo I presumed, but no unless it was a hell of a long pee, something else was brewing.

Lo and behold, 'Maureeeece' reappears dressed in a Tarzan outfit. Like I said, he had the physique for it and instantly became the center of attention. Everyone is in fits, especially the invited dignitaries, and I am left standing there, wishing I had the balls to be an extrovert.

How much guts does it take to pull off a stunt like that? An obvious rebel, a man who could not only mix it with the best of them in the Officers mess but also give a one-fingered salute whenever he felt the need. Well, this was my interpretation of his performance, when in fact, the real reason was a whole lot simpler.

Several weeks on, another port, another cocktail party, and 'Maureeeece' follows where he left off. Guests find it hilarious. The rest of us find it very funny. Next port, hysterics from one group and more 'Ho-hum' from the other. By the fourth time, I am left thinking, 'Right, come on, pack it in for god's sake or at least change the outfit,' and by the fifth, the general consensus is to have him thrown overboard once we set sail.

By this time, most of us would make our excuses after an hour and leave to avoid the sideshow. It had become embarrassingly predictable. Here was a man that did not just like attention.

He needed it. The stupid name, the physique, the perma-tan, and that bloody Tarzan outfit. By the time the official tour nearing its completion, the place usually scattered whenever Maureeece now walked into the Officer's mess. Funny how the milk always turns sour.

Unlike my appreciation of the odd bit of attention now and again, narcissists are attention junkies. It's been said they are usually larger than life characters, but I'm not sure I entirely agree with this. No doubt Maureeeece certainly was, but Sarah's unfortunate choice of partner was most definitely not.

Okay, he's a fictional character, but my point was to get across that although personalities can vary, ultimately, they have this capacity to draw us in, grabbing our attention in the first place irrespective of how over the top they might be. So what's the secret?

Narcissists will be thrilled to hear that studies continually show that, as a group, they are usually rated more attractive and likable than everyone else on first appearances. Not only are they shits, but they are attractive shits into the bargain. Who said life is fair?

Women who score highly on tests of narcissism consistently dress more provocatively than their more modest counterparts. This was certainly the case with the author's personal experience in Glasgow. She blew me away before blowing me off the park sometime later.

The men are usually more stylish. The clothes are made to fit rather than just hanging off the shoulder, [no danger of me being a narcissist then] cheerful, and just more physically appealing than those scoring lower on the tests. In essence, they just happen to be very good at catching the eye in the first place. After that, it's on to stage two.

It is worth mentioning that being a narcissist does not come cheap, which partly explains their propensity for being so selfish. They will always let someone else pay the bill, put petrol in the car, buy a round, etc., unless they have a plan, i.e., are trying to impress or are chatting you up.

But after that, they become incredibly stingy, except with themselves. Heaven forbid they are seen in the same outfit too often, or the car becomes dated. No, no, no, image for a narcissist is everything, as it brings attention.

As the partner of a narcissist, your role is effectively that of being an unpaid prop. Firstly you will have to look good, that's why you were chosen in the first place, alongside your undoubted people-pleasing abilities.

Looking so good on their arm draws even more attention in their direction [remember Chris asking Sarah to tart it up a bit in the pizza restaurant] and woe betides if you let standards slip. You will be reminded in no uncertain terms that this will not be tolerated.

This will probably be phrased subtly, to begin with, becoming blunter as time goes on. Again, referring back to the story by example, you will recall our characters' first party. On the drive there, Chris was his usual miserable and taciturn self. Still, on arrival, DA-NAAA, it became showtime, and he, chameleon-like, adapted his persona to one of a social, gregarious, and loving partner. No pat on the thigh driving there, but my goodness, he made up for it at the party. Very touchy-feely, with an arm around the waist, especially when he could sniff a photo opportunity coming up.

Boasting is also de rigeur with narcissists. Partners always know the truth, of course, but you just have to grin and bear it as they always overplay their financial capacity or sporting prowess. Nods of loving approval mean less of a hard time when you get back in the car.

The one thing they have no control over, well, unless they are minted and can afford a decent plastic surgeon [and narcissists will always consider surgery], is time. For a narcissist, their greatest enemy is age. It is harder to create the wow factor with a receding hairline, potbelly, and a turkey neck. But they will always try hard.

Even if, as a couple, you can't afford the electricity bill, the narcissist will always find a way to justify that new purchase, that trendy haircut, those new teeth, or breast implants. And they tend to keep themselves in shape longer than the rest of us as they love going to the gym—a great way to get noticed as a reward for all the hours spent on the treadmill.

Forgive me another anecdote, but as the subject matter is attention, it lends itself superbly to the observational stuff.

Like most people, I do my weekly food shopping on a certain day, at a certain time. Saturday mornings, to be precise, quite early, before the screaming families turn up and monopolize the cereal aisles. Always the same supermarket, not a hypermarket but one of the well-known discount varieties, of a certain size and limited range. Two syllables if you need a further clue.

Other creatures of habit shop here at the same time as me, so I guess in a very loose kind of way, we're all observing, noticing little nuances here and there. And you know what it's like, sometimes you just get a feeling about somebody, without actually knowing them. For example, two fellow shoppers have always held my interest. No doubt they also have their radar on others, but as a two or three out of ten, I doubt it's me. To avoid accusations of bias, luckily, one is male and the other female.

Let's start with the bloke. He'll be around his mid-sixties, I guess, over six feet, and he has this air of confidence about him, not so much a walk, more a swagger, not quite John Wayne, but you get the gist. Chin up, head always held high kind of thing.

Actually, he reminds me of an aging roadie stereotype. Still got the long hair, albeit straggly and grey down the sides but bald on top, think Friar Tuck lookalike but with long hair, ear-ring, and beer belly. It's this swagger he has, where he thinks he can still cut it.

Occasionally, in the checkout queue, he'll do that tossing of the head thing, brushing the hair to the side with his hand, while catching his reflection in the mirrored office glass window behind.

He's always immaculately dressed for nine o'clock on a Saturday morning, whereas his wife, well, I assume it is his wife, follows on behind pushing the trolley, looking the way most of us do at that time. Funnily enough, yes, she always follows from behind, never in front. I've even loitered in the car park to see who loads the shopping into the boot. Need any guesses?

Now, I don't know if this guy is a narcissist, but he sure as hell sends out the signals. I wish I knew his name? The need to be noticed, the dress sense and the way he acts, a kind of aloofness with the staff [who you suspect all the time are laughing behind his back].

He does have a seriously annoying habit of being in the queue and disputing prices, which of course, lengthens the queue and pisses the rest of us off. Of course, that then brings additional attention, but what does he care? It's all about him.

The second example is a completely different kettle of fish, and to me seems a much nicer person. We always say our hello's, never got round to pleasantries yet, but a hello is more than I get from the other bloke. I have tried twice, but why would a narcissist bother as a male with nothing to offer?] Am guessing she's in her mid to late fifties and is the complete opposite of Mr. Aging Roadie.

She's still lovely, with the kind of features that make you think, boy, I'll bet she turned a few heads in her time. But does she look as if she spends an hour and a half in the bathroom on a Saturday morning before coming out to spend a quarter of her wages on the weekly food shop? No way!

There she is, the spitting image of a Greenham Common protestor, all pink wellies with blue polka dots and hair all over the place. She always has a smile, is incredibly courteous, and knows most of the staff by name—the type of person whose partner is very, very lucky to have her.

The point of these two examples, if you haven't already figured it out, is that the non-narcissist accepts the aging process. I mean, who the hell wants to embrace getting old? It is just that non-narcissists accept that's life, and get on with other things instead, always being the better person for it, whereas the narcissists seem to keep hanging on in there thinking they still 'cut it' when it's obvious they don't. They somehow always manage to come across as being not quite so nice.

You will not be surprised to hear that staff think nothing of opening another till for the pink wellied customer if they see her waiting too long in the queue. I wonder what they think of me, other than why does that man keep staring at us?

Forgive me for my slight transgression, but you can see I have a thing about aging narcissists.

So, let's get back to the here and now. I have explained how they hook your attention in the first place, so now onto Stage two of their game plan, which involves holding onto the attention and then milking it to death. I'll be discussing attention within the context of narcissists as friends a few chapters down the line, so, for now, it's simply attention from the angle of a romantic interest I'll examine.

In the early days [quite literally], it is the narcissist making all the sacrifices. They see this as a short-term investment for considerable reward further down the line. If they did not see the potential reward, they simply wouldn't waste their time. Think back to the early days of Chris and Sarah.

He hooked her in with his looks, charm and charisma before hitting her with the love bombing. She must have thought all her Xmas's had come at once, with the attention he lavished so generously, by way of continual phone calls, texts, meals out and weekends away and all with the promise of yet more to come.

This is crucial, for once they know they have you snared, the initial investment is terminated, and they begin to back off, leaving you to do all the running [giving attention] praying to god that they don't now pack you in.

By dishing out healthy doses of the silent treatment now and again, this serves to fuel your paranoia [as well as exert control, of course] that the relationship may be on the wane, so once more, you up the ante with making contact [i.e., even more attention coming their way].

Are you getting the gist of how the system now works? Think of it as the person who cares least about the relationship holding all the power. This is narcissists to a tee. The good news, though, is that they can be outmaneuvered, more of that in the chapter 'Can narcissists be out—narcissised?'

The roles have been firmly established since the testing period, and yours is now one of narcissistic supply, which is giving attention to a partner on a positive, reliable and regular basis. Top-up attention through encouragement, motivation, shoulder to cry on, etc., will be required when their supply levels from elsewhere become depleted.

In other words, when they have hacked everyone else off! It's up to you to massage their ego that it's everyone else in the wrong and not them. The flipside to this is that when things are going well for the narcissist, excessive congratulatory attention [bordering on adulation] will also be required to remind them how wonderful they are. Phew, talk about having your cake and eating it.

But just as things are going so selfishly well for them, they go and do what narcissists always do when things go their way. They fuck it all up by becoming bored. Age may be their physical enemy, but complacency and boredom are their mental nemesis.

They always get bored. They get bored of you, they get bored with their friends and then, of course, there's their job. Not all simultaneously, of course, but look on it as one big narcissistic conveyor belt, where new sources of attention are added as the existing ones become stale, no longer providing the hit to the ego they once found so satisfying.

Assuming they can just flit in and out of people's lives as the mood takes them, the narcissist learns, to their cost, that life, unfortunately, does not quite work that way. Being used as a glorified stage prop is not everyone's cup of tea.

Once the 'safe bets' go on the wane, there's usually a valiant attempt to take up where they left off, but, by now, it has become a case of too little, too late. For friends, it may be that the narcissist will revisit some of the restaurants you once frequented on the off chance you just happen to bump into one another.

Or, in Sarah's case, when the charm offensive no longer works, the darker Machiavellian side springs into action, and he goads her to give him the attention he so desperately craves.

For the record, the character's story was based on the experiences of two close friends who were both in long-term relationships with narcissists, and their exploits are about as close to the story as I could manage.

As for 'Maureeece', we only sailed together with them once, so I'll never know how he behaved on other ships, but I can hazard a guess. Somewhere out there on the high seas, flying the flag on behalf of the British Empire, a wrinkled old Tarzan will be plying his trade.

CHAPTER 6

NARCISSISTS AND CONTROL

They say if you wonder whether or not you're a narcissist, then you are probably not. But even the most ardent of narcissist spotters [such as myself] can still have our doubts. We all possess narcissistic personality traits to varying degrees. If sixteen percent of the population are meant to be narcissistic, that equates to odds around one in six that you, me, or someone very close by will indeed be a narcissist.

So, what were the alarm bells that fueled my paranoia? For starters, I have a terrible attention span. This in itself is not a defining character trait, but the tendency to become bored very easily usually follows on, and that certainly is.

This could explain my frequent career changes, another defining character trait, alongside the tendency to be obsessive, which is quite high on the O.C.D scale. Not, I hasten to add, that all the tins have to be facing the same way in the kitchen cupboard kind of thing.

I have to do more embarrassing little things in a particular order, or else I believe I'll come a cropper. So far, so bad, right? Add in the odd white lie now and again [minor manipulation] and an occasional touch of arrogance, and you appreciate more why I've had my doubts. So what's the saving grace? Lack of vanity?

Hardly. How can you be vain at my age, with a bald head and designer stubble that's become a darker shade of grey? If

I succumbed to a hair transplant and then bought beard dye, that would be an altogether different story, right? No, I'll tell you where my savior lies, being well outside the danger zone for the top two defining characteristics of narcissism, i.e., attention and control.

Without these two characteristics, you may, like me, occasionally think you are narcissistic, but chances are, you won't even come close. I do not know anyone with an abundance of traits that do not equal the other.

Understandably, it's the attention-seeking charisma from the narcissist that hooks you in the first place. But that's just to soften you up before the control tactics start with a vengeance. Scoring myself so poorly on the attention front, I'll go even lower with control.

Heck, with my people-pleasing tendencies, I am so far the other way I'm not sure I would even make it onto the point's ladder. I have more experience of being controlled than being the controller. Attention has been covered, so now let's look at 'Control'.

For any victim coming out of a toxic relationship, to hear claims of the abusive partner as being overbearing or controlling. It's sometimes difficult to comprehend how anyone could tolerate a partner behaving this way, and I can only explain this by saying that you will never quite know unless you have been there.

Half the time, being so eager to please the narcissistic partner since they are so cunning and plausible, you become so conditioned that you are unaware of being controlled in the first place. You just accept the situation as being the norm. Every one of your questions has a rational response. Any doubts are met with a disbelieving shake of the head or a reminder of your capacity to blow things out of proportion. You are accused of being paranoid if you mention you think they are controlling you. 'Take a look in the mirror they frequently say' and 'a bit more appreciation would not go amiss', from you, not them.

Narcissists have an underlying need to control everyone in their environment, partners, work colleagues, friends, neighbors, and even pets. I kid you not. Take time out to think of anyone you know that is narcissistic and think of their choice of pet. Is it dog or cat? The dog usually wins hands down as they can be controlled. When was the last time you managed to control a cat?

Narcissists see everyone in their environment as extensions of themselves but with them firmly in the driving seat running the show. An idol is admired by their subjects beneath, where control is exerted by charisma, manipulation, coercion, or just plain bullying to keep their subjects in line.

This is critical, as it allows the narcissist to go off sowing their seeds or having fun elsewhere, safe in the knowledge that the old faithfuls will still be hanging around when they get back. Lack of loyalty is never tolerated.

Before we get to the relationship aspect of control, let me share with you an experience of mine with a narcissistic work colleague, which epitomizes the behavior perfectly.

I started a new job a short while back, and you know what it was like in the early days. I was feeling a bit uncertain and trying to settle in as quickly as I could. Everyone was friendly, but there's always the one who isn't there, someone who wants you to know just how new you are. And you should know your place. This was a woman in her mid-forties, a very authoritative character, and even without a chain of command,

I could see fellow staff members and even some management kind of deferring to her.

This was a different version of my naval days all over again. Whereas 'Maureeeece' needed attention and controlled everyone by charm into achieving this, this new woman was the same, except she bullied everyone into submission.

I knew within five minutes of meeting her that a day of reckoning between us was inevitable. This woman played the control card to a tee, always wangling something or someone to achieve favored status.

Of course, being a new boy, I became the number one target. Firstly, it was the swapping of shift, in her favor, of course, which I willingly went along with. From that, she then asked, as we lived relatively near each other if I wouldn't mind giving her a lift to work. Of course, I agreed, but by now, a distinct pattern has emerged, that of one-way traffic.

Now, any normal, level-headed person would recognize a generous person when they saw one and reciprocate accordingly. But no, this is a narcissist we're talking about, and her thought processes would be something along the lines of 'this person is just so dumb and inferior he deserves to be taken advantage of, and that's just what I'm going to do...'. So was I doing her a disservice by second-guessing her motives? No, because off she went and behaved as per the script. This was her very own 'Testing Period,' and I passed with flying colors.

It was then a request to give her a lift home from work from giving her a lift to work. Hell, I even went home via a McDonalds one night, as she fancied a burger! By now, I am feeling resentful and used. Others might say 'mug' was stamped on my forehead. It gets worse. She then starts more or less telling me the pickup time.

By now, my 'blood boiling' pressure gauge is firmly in the red. One day she just pushed her luck too far, and I finally let rip Arrrgggggghhhhhhhhh!!!!! No messing about, no diplomacy, I just went for her, all guns blazing. Boy, did it feel good. Letting rip with a narcissist when there's no emotional connection does wonders for the psyche!

Now I completely accept that I should have nipped this in the bud a long time before and been a bit more rational in explaining my feelings.

Still, some of us have this capacity, and some of us don't, but on the other hand, when does being rational ever work with a narcissist because all they do is come back a short while later but with a different strategy.

My outburst served its purpose, more so in fact, as other colleagues gained confidence and started 'taking her on', which of course, resulted in a complete loss of face. As narcissists are bullies and bullies have chronically low self-esteem, her embarrassment at losing top dog status would have been palpable. She resigned a short while after, and the change in atmosphere was instant. Dark clouds now sat elsewhere in the city.

Not that I enjoy dealing with narcissists at the best of times, more so now that I am older, wiser, and some might even say bitter.

Not for me to comment on that one, but I'd still rather deal with them in the context of work colleagues or friends simply because there's still that emotional distance or at the very least a loose connection which can still be severed without it having anywhere near the same impact as that of a relationship. No skin off my nose if I never see that woman again or the fact that I was to sail with 'Maureeece' just the once.

For the record, some two months after she resigned, she came back cap in hand, asking for her old job back. No doubt her new employer was less tolerant of her antics. She was unsuccessful. As for the control tactics friends employ, the chapter 'Narcissists as friends' follows shortly, but rest assured, they too always seem to come a cropper. There are those in life that never seem to know just when they are onto a good thing.

Right, so let's get into relationships.

The halcyon phase is over, and there have been a few blips here and there, little tests along the way to see if fair game, and then the big test came along, which you passed with flying colors. You are now totally besotted with your narcissistic partner and fully compliant with their requests. [Or to describe it in layman's terms, continually giving in to their nonsense]

The narcissist's first critical stage of control is to distance their partner from all available support networks.

Remember how in the early days, your intention for a night out with friends would be met with 'but we hardly see each other as it is...' or, 'but honey, I had something planned...'

Well, now the same request will either be met with accusations of your selfishness [it's all about you being there twenty-four seven for your partner] or, more likely, a healthy dose of the silent treatment so that you know how angry you have made them. So two to three-day 'huffs' will not be uncommon.

The fewer people you have to confide in, the more benefit of the doubt will become the order of the day. You will, of course, be allowed the odd night out with friends, but only those friends that meet the narcissist's criteria, i.e., they are as susceptible as you. They also have to be fans of the narcissist because if not, they are out.

Once the wagons are circled, isolation takes hold, which leads nicely to the next stage, erosion of confidence. Those little quirks and mannerisms you have, part and parcel of what makes us all so unique in the first place, will be pointed out and magnified. Of course, phrased in such a way that 'they are only trying to help' or 'to make you a better person'.

Narcissists are masters at instilling self-doubt. Therein lies the irony, although feelings of insecurity and self-doubt themselves plague them, they belittle even further those people they deem inferior -i.e., friendly people, who are way too accommodating for their good. Once they have eroded their partner's confidence by constant belittling, then it's a job well done for the narcissist. Always better for their ego to be a big fish in a very, very small pond

But now you are wisening up and becoming aware of their Machiavellian ways. Things being no longer quite what they seem from the earlier days. The same predicament as Sarah, your role is now that of the actor taking on whatever is necessary to fulfill their needs. Think back to one of their final social events as a couple.

Being controlled by the silent treatment on the way there, a case of only speaking when spoken to but then showered with affection once the show hit the road.

From being ignored, half an hour earlier, she became top of his pedestal and had to act accordingly lest risking the wrath of narcissist Chris if something were said out of place. She still had to don another hat before the night drew to a close, that of the great provider of moral support.

Yes, his stories were the most entertaining, and yes, he was easily the most popular man there, and on and on it goes. One wonders if Tina Turner's 'Simply the Best' has its origins in being written for a narcissistic partner. I mean, who would write that title for someone under normal circumstances?

So you've lost half your friends, and your confidence is being eroded by the day. It kind of irritates the shit out of you that your family still thinks this partner is the best thing to come into your life in a long time, but maybe they are right. I mean, if they thought otherwise, they would tell you, right? No wrong. It is that they are being charmed and controlled as well. It is just that you will figure it all out well before they do.

Unable to make decisions without their approval, not only have you become compliant, but you are increasingly mentally dependent on them. What happened to the well-grounded, happy with their lot person that went into this relationship with their eyes wide open? Where have they gone? Everyone else is wondering the same.

You seem to receive a heck of many texts and mobile calls from your partner at work. 'Where are you?' 'When are you coming home?' 'I need this...' 'Can you get me that...?' Some days it's endless, and it's not gone unnoticed at work.

You now appear edgy and always seem to be in a rush. Colleagues can see you become visibly anxious when you hear the ringtone. Forget Friday night drinks with everyone after work. Those days have well and truly gone. You see yourself as weak and hate yourself for it. Shit, now there's self-loathing to contend with.

Your job has become an increasingly no-win situation. You are either accused of spending too much time with your work at the expense of the relationship or too little time out earning when all these bills are paid. How can you win? The answer is you can't, but it is all about instilling self-doubt. Continually questioning yourself increases your reliance on them which fuels dependency, which finally leads to control. Get it?

As always, there will be the occasional praise [just to keep you wrong footed], but you now treat these backhanded compliments with the contempt they deserve. If only you could leave this shit of a partner' but you need them, and they like to remind you just how much. 'After everything I do, you wouldn't last two minutes without me...' Sound familiar?

You still like to try and look good for your partner, anything to score brownie points, but that's now become a complete no-win. Always so critical, on the one hand, they want you to be sexy or smart, then on the other, give you the silent treatment when you get attention from elsewhere.

To alleviate the silences, you find yourself apologizing for a lot, which they duly accept until they decide it's time you were put back in that little box of yours all over again. You know yourself this cannot continue, or you'll become a nervous wreck.

So at some point or another, you finally wake up and smell the roses. Remember what happened to Sarah, it might not be all of them at once, but I'd bet there are a few in there you can relate to, infidelity being the usual candidate. 'It was just the once darling', 'a moment of madness', 'It was you, you stopped being nice to me, you made me do it'.

Ring any bells? A dog can only take a kicking for so long before it bites back, so you call it a day. Then guess what? If they can't control you from the inside, then they'll go hammer and tong to control from the outside to coerce you back into the fold. Abandoning a narcissist is a big no-no unless it's on their terms, of course, so now they try and force themselves back into your life.

To begin with, it's an attempt at revisiting the love-bombing Idealisation phase. Flowers, gifts, invitations to dinner, in essence, everything bar the kitchen sink is thrown in your direction to validate just how much of a great partner they truly are, and look at what you could be losing out on should you metaphorically kiss them goodbye.

This won't work, of course. You're a bit too battle-hardened by now to fall for this shit, so nope, it is now onto the much harder part, which requires a great deal more effort than a common or garden phone call to the local florist.

As per the storyline, they will now resort to turning up unannounced at your home or work, your favorite Bar or Restaurant, the local Supermarket, in a nutshell anywhere you frequent, which may result in the obligatory 'chance' encounter.

Hand in hand comes stalking. Rest assured they will be parked up nearby or standing somewhere within watching distance of activities. Will you be aware of this? Of course, you will, but without the concrete evidence to prove it. Still, a form of control is being planted firmly inside your grey matter, showing just how unlikely it is that they will be moving on anytime soon. But they do, eventually.

But the whole drawn-out saga can take months at the earliest or years at the latest. Sorry about that one. Oh, and don't forget, as a parting shot, they'll still throw in a decent smear campaign for good measure, anything to discredit your reputation and disturb the psyche. Hell hath no fury and all that!

A final point to consider and look on this as a general rule of thumb.

Once you begin to feel you are being used and begin to doubt yourself, you are already in too deep.

CHAPTER 7

NARCISSISTS AS FRIENDS

Allow me, if you will, a moment of self-indulgence. Let's talk about me. After all, it is a book on narcissism, but this is more to do with articulating thoughts than anything to do with self-promotion.

So, as a regular, middle-aged, been around the block, kind of guy, how do I look upon friendship in general terms? What does it mean to me? What do I get out of it?

There are three categories of friends in my own life—regular [usually due to proximity], work-related friends, and seeing each other once in a blue moon kind of friends, again usually distance affected.

What I get from each group is ultimately feeling comfortable in their company, with a loose form of emotional connection. In layman's terms, this is usually [but not always] seen as being on the same wavelength. There have never seemed to be any moments of real elation, nor any spats that led to a serious confrontation, the ship always seeming to sail on an even keel. These are people I trust, and I just feel comfortable being around them.

As my work friends are the ones I will see most often, my spirits are raised when I see our shift patterns coinciding. At an unconscious level, I am sure my blood pressure and general well-being are improved from spending time in their company.

I like to think this is a two-way street. There are no bucket loads of cortisol or adrenaline being released into my bloodstream in the company of these people. I general terms, does this kind of seem normal, fair, reasonable, a nice position? I think so. Maybe I could do better, but who knows? I am perfectly content with what I have.

As I write and both think at the same time, I am asking myself if there is any common denominator that distinguished these people, the ones whom I regard as friends, from the others, who seemed to tick all the right boxes at the start, but fell by the wayside, some leaving a feeling of intense dislike.

Yes, one simple fact—these people all just grew on me. There was no instant chemistry, no immediate rapport. It is simple, as each week and month passed by, we began to like each other just that little but more, building mutual trust along the way. On a purely personal basis, I cannot think of anyone who made a terrific first impression which has come anywhere close to standing the test of time.

The counter-argument is that I am just picky—but, with zero exceptions, the individuals in question who held such great promise [and we're now talking the narcissistic art of the great first impression] have also been given short shrift by others.

Sometime's you just get a feeling with some people that things are simply not meant to be. With no emotional connection, it's a thousand times easier just to let go than hang around waiting for things to improve.

But narcissists do not have this view of friendship. They cannot feel empathy and will not do anything unless of benefit to themselves. They want new friends, but only if they can get something from them, and existing friends slowly slide down the pecking order of importance once someone of more superior credentials comes along.

That said, narcissists need people the same way the rest of us need oxygen to survive. In essence, we are their life supply. Just like our fictitious character Sarah in earlier chapters, being bowled over by narcissistic charm in the early days, the same criteria apply when we meet narcissists as potential friends.

The paradox is that they may be superb at winning us over in the short term, but, in the long run, the wheels will always come off. Even the most forgiving and patient souls will eventually decide enough is enough and move on to new pastures. And so the charm offensive begins afresh with new people, and the script repeated.

It must be arduous work being a narcissist. One would assume that eventually, the penny would drop that a different approach would reap substantially better rewards, but narcissists don't do self-awareness very well.

So, how do narcissists as friends operate in practice?

I see it as more or less the same format as Sarah went through, just without the lovemaking.

Everything is a stage, a predictable format. There will be nothing dramatic, just little things that, taken together, make the friendship untenable. By way of an easy example, if I had a friend of particular political leanings [and most do] who one day decided to go off and form an extreme right-wing Fascist party, I'm sure I would choose there and then, 'Right, that's it, I'm off byeee.'

But narcissists are a lot more subtle, at least initially. It's never until you have forgiven several disappointments that they will decide to up the ante and crank up the notch just a little bit more each time.

No doubt, this acquaintanceship got off to a good start. We're all suckers for anyone who can make an entrance, and a narcissist is usually superb at getting off to a flying start, whether through looks, humor, or charisma. One way or another, there will be something that draws you in. They usually seem to have lots of friends, and you can understand why.

Being in the company of someone so popular makes you feel good about yourself. It rubs off. 'Heh, if they really like me, and they already have lots of friends, then surely I must be a good person worth knowing?'

Already this is a win-win. Everyone is feeling great, and to begin with, you will see rather a lot of each other. Again, just as with poor old Sarah, your new friends will be taking note of all your likes and dislikes, either stored in the mental recess or even written down, lest they forget. This is very important because if this friendship gathers pace, it means you are very high up in their hierarchy of potential great friends.

You see, to get to this stage, you must have fulfilled specific criteria, the main one being your usefulness to them because a} you have something they want and b} you are probably a lovely person.

This hierarchy stuff is pretty straightforward. It is based on your value to them—be it looks [pretty crucial considering how vain they are themselves] status [vital considering how successful they see themselves compared to ordinary mortals] or money [needless to say hugely, stratospherically important considering the number freebies that could be winging their way to them once you realize you cannot afford not to have them as friends].

If you have all these, you win the jackpot and will be wined, dined, and initially worshiped. So far, so good, right? Well, yes, they are great company, their opinions, likes, and dislikes echo your own, and it is always easier to be with people naturally in tune with the life you lead yourself. I was close to describing them as empathic, but no, that is not a word you can ever use to describe a narcissist. More on that to follow.

Everything is great, unless, that is, you are the poor sod who's just been demoted because someone new and better has appeared on the scene. Sorry, old chuck, but my narcissistic energies are now being diverted elsewhere. The very people who were once in your position and have been used to expending vast amounts of their time, energy, and, no doubt money, to maintain this friendship can be demoted in the blink of an eye.

There is never any remorse. That's just the way it goes. Now, of course, because narcissists never explain anything honestly or adequately, the previous friends, if they are big on forgiveness and are still hanging on, will be left perplexed and wondering why the phone never rings.

But back to the here and now, where you are basking in the glory of this fantastic new friendship! There is always a witty line awaiting your arrival or a wave across the restaurant to some fellow diners as you take your seats. God, these guys are so popular, and they have chosen us to dine with. How good are we?

What will become apparent is just how much this couple loves being together after all these years. There will be plenty of eye contact, they will be touchy-feely, and she will still seem to hang on his every word. Goodness will seem to emanate from every orifice of their being.

It will be clear just how much you have in common. And it will also be made clear how successful they are. Of course, they will always avoid specifics, but you will be gently probed on details of your situation. This is more useful to them than to reveal the kind of stuff about themselves which could likely trip them up later.

The wooing they do as friends is very similar to the courting they do in romantic relationships. They will be careful to 'mirror' your thoughts and views so that you think you have a lot in common. They will ask you a lot of questions. Don't be flattered—this is just, so they have useful information—partly for this mirroring, but partly so they have information on your weaknesses and foibles they can use against you if needs be.

While all this is going on, one will take the lead in all discussions, highlighting their successes and talents. You will be allowed to participate but in a much more minor way.

Your accomplishments will never match theirs. They are a golden couple in every way, including their love for each other. You will be allowed to bask in the knowledge that this couple has chosen you as friends, and you should feel privileged. At the outset, much as with romantic relationships, the parallels are uncanny.

At the end of the meal, Mr. Narcissist will insist on paying but no, no, you're having none of that, and insist on paying your share, which he grudgingly accepts. This is a tactic that always works.

He knows you're a nice couple and would feel guilty about accepting his offer, so he plays his initial generosity card. This will be followed by the 'Believe me, I really don't mind' card, which, of course, does that little bit more to win over your trust.

Several get-togethers will follow over the coming few months and will follow the same pattern. But then, as with Sarah, when they decide you are truly committed, the nonsense will start.

This is always by way of subtle tests. The first one is usually timekeeping. That tried and tested favorite. Narcissists will always stick to what they know. As I said, the script never changes.

It will seem inconsequential to start with, but those little fifteen minutes late will gradually develop into half hours or hours. There will always be a plausible excuse—lost car keys, traffic, always explained away with a humorous anecdote. Now, you are either the type to accept this, or you are not. If you are, you can justify it in your mind by recalling how busy they are.

This is another facet of the narcissistic couple and their frantically busy lifestyle. As the conversations develop, you will find yourself talking less and listening more. The chat will become more one-sided.

There will be the occasional opportunity to share your news, but this will happen less. The charm and wit will still be evident, but you will find yourself becoming increasingly annoyed at how picky they now seem to be. The restaurant table will be unsuitable. They will demand another. It will either be draughty or too warm.

Watch out for complaints about dirty cutlery or food that has to be sent back. Of course, this will not happen all at once—just enough to become routine and slightly embarrassing. If they become aware they are pushing their luck, and you are getting annoyed, the nonsense will temporarily stop, and they will revert to the original charm and fun that won you over in the first place.

Ringing any bells yet?

Status is vital to narcissists. Rest assured, wherever you are planning to go this year, they will either have been, or it will be in the pipeline. They will either have a similar size or quickly upgraded with your car, lest they feel inferior.

As for occupation, the narcissist must be doing something as worthy as you, which is part of the reason you were selected in the first place. They will usually have just started in the new position and will be vague on the specifics, just in case you already know someone in that field. If only you knew!

But of course, with friendships, the benefits of doubt are not as prolonged as in love relationships.

But new friendships are like new relationships, with the capacity to reinvigorate so that misgivings will be overlooked and transgressions are forgiven. Progressing from evenings out, the relationship can move onto day trips or weekends away. If you make it to this stage, you have potential—but check who does most of the organizing.

Narcissists are great with the ideas and entertainment but not so hot on the actual mechanics of making things happen.

This is where you come in. The boring stuff—that's for you to sort out. If payment is required up front, don't expect their share to be forthcoming immediately.

Maybe the first time, but embarrassing [for you], gentle reminders will be required after that. By this stage, you will be arriving home very puzzled. 'Is it me...? Did you notice...? or Do you get the feeling...?' It will become common. All the while, they will continue to be great company, but something won't feel quite right about this pair. Something just doesn't add up. The jigsaw is incomplete.

There is always a more dominant partner in a narcissistic couple, while the more subservient one plays the ball to get an easier life. Since like attracts like, they must have had characteristics that drew them together in the first place but referring back to Chapters 1-3, there is always one more dominant with the other knowing their place.

The purpose of mentioning this is to be clear who the top dog is by this time. The one that does the bragging, the one that demands attention, and must be pitied for being a precise number two. It's the role of the number two to act as the pacifist, the peacemaker when they see that number one is beginning to irritate others in company. Occasionally, the guard will drop [courtesy of alcohol], and the façade will crack. The truth slowly but surely emerges from the shadows.

The erratic lifestyle and compromised finances begin to show a picture far removed from the one initially presented to the world, but they still go along with the show. Why? It might be a case of 'Better the devil you know,' or it might be that all eggs are in one basket, and there is no place left to go. And boy, will they be reminded of this regularly.

You take pity and soldier on, usually for the sake of the downtrodden partner, but increasingly it begins to grate. With your generosity of spirit now taken for granted, arrogance and complacency now become the order of the day. A night out at the movies—and guess who will feel entitled to talk throughout. There may be disparaging remarks about mutual acquaintances. They may cancel events at short notice or not bother turning up.

Likewise, getting a better offer at the last minute and accepting it is not uncommon narcissistic behavior. Like a selfish schoolchild with a friend who has a free cinema ticket, they will think nothing of leaving behind their other friend whom they had promised to play football.

Narcissists have absolutely no empathy. They cannot put themselves in someone else's shoes, so they cannot understand why someone would be upset. Like the child letting down his friend, his behavior has been allowed to continue through adolescence and into adulthood, so do not ever expect a miraculous transformation. It is simply never going to happen.

All will indicate that boredom has kicked in on their part. In all probability, new friends are being cultivated elsewhere for their usefulness. Should you have the audacity to challenge their behavior, the chief narcissist will become moody or confrontational.

All narcissists suffer from debilitatingly low self-esteem. They will try to keep this hidden, but it manifests in how they react to criticism and pulls up some of their behavior. They take it to heart, becoming hurt and feeling rejection very strongly.

By now, with so many red flags waving, you realize the friendship is fast approaching its conclusion. The rose-tinted glasses are long gone, and their true colors are showing. Complete self-absorption is the most annoying trait. Absolutely everything is about them.

For sure, you feel pity for the downtrodden partner, but they can still do a good turn at their version of selfishness, greed, and manipulation. All this effort at maintaining a one-sided friendship brings little by way of joy.

Choosing to remain friends with a narcissist requires strong self-esteem and the ability to draw a line in the sand as regards healthy boundaries, which are never crossed, ever.

On a personal note, I find it easier to ditch these people when part of a couple. It is easier to bounce feelings off one another [Did I imagine that...?...am I overreacting..?] There is strength in mutual support. Being on your own becomes harder simply because you lack the initial feedback, which can make the difference between hanging around and heading for the hills.

Ask yourself what you get out of this friendship. Feeling used all the time does nothing for your mental well-being. Your self-esteem becomes deflated, which then affects other parts of your life. The head can drop when these feelings become the norm, and gradually giving in to people becomes the norm. Adopt a mantra of three strikes, and you are out.

Once a friend lets you down on three occasions with no valid reason, or one that's a bit stale, get rid of them. Look at the first letdown as a 'well, these things can happen' moment. The subsequent disappointment can be classed as your 'giving them the benefit of the doubt' moment. The final one will be the 'you know what, now you're taking the piss' conclusion.

It won't be long till someone else is in your shoes. Bear in mind the world can be a small place for those who take liberties with forgiveness. Eventually, these types develop a reputation where options become increasingly thin on the ground.

The very fact that you find yourself in this position and asking these questions means you know what you should be doing anyway.

Subsequent chapters go into more detail about narcissist spotting but remember [and I will keep repeating this until you become fed up hearing] they will never change. So when your antennae start flashing, drop them like a brick. The world is full of much nicer people, just dying to meet someone like you.

CHAPTER 8

HOW COULD I HAVE BEEN SO STUPID?

How often have we asked ourselves that question? How about that sure-fire stock market investment, or that bargain-basement holiday with spectacular sea views, or that friend of a friend who does plumbing on the side for cash? Yep, we've all been there. You know what it's like, those golden opportunities to save a few quid or make a killing before everyone else does.

Somehow it always seems to cloud our better judgment and very nearly lose the shirts off our backs in the process. There is always time to draw out at the very last minute and save our skin, though, that niggling little doubt at the back of the mind that won't disappear, fueled by the advice of that sensible friend who never seems to come a cropper in the way we do.

But no, we plow on. With that delusional, don't worry. Things will work out fine in the end approach. We only have ourselves to blame in the end.

What about relationships? Any daft mistakes there? How about in the early days, the thrill of dating some bad boys or sexy girls, the kind that makes your heart skip a beat and your mother roll her eyes in equal measure? They never last very long, do they, but guess what, you go out and do the same thing all over again.

At least by now, you have some experience in the bag to fall back on. For sure, you know it won't last, but sometimes having someone is better than having no one at all, and you won't be crying into your pillow this time when it all goes pear-shaped.

Want any more?

What about an affair? That must be high up there when people ask themselves afterward how they could have been so dumb. The initial excitement of the illicit affair, only for heartbreak to follow when things go belly up, and the front door gets kicked in by jealous spouse as the optional extra. Now, that is dumb!

But what if I was to tell you that there's even worse than that? I mean, what if I were to suggest that there are some sensible middle-aged people out there who allow themselves to fall for someone and, in the process, succumb to becoming so controlled and manipulated that they are powerless to prevent it?

I mean, could you ever imagine yourself allowing that? Thought not, but you accept the fact that sometimes weak-willed people allow themselves to get in too deep for their good.

But no, not you! You're smarter than that, right? Okay, so if that were not bad enough, how about if I suggest that these same unfortunates will be prepared to pack in their jobs, friends, and family, and even hand over everything they have, just to be with this person, and even then feel as if it is not enough, that they have to continually do more lest they lose this love of their life. Could you ever imagine yourself doing that? Are you kidding me? It is the terse reply! Nice to know you consider yourself so mentally assertive.

The bad news is that some people will do precisely that. These are not academically stupid individuals or people lacking in self-belief.

Experience in life is everything, and we rarely make the same mistakes twice, But just when you think you have reached a certain age and got a handle on the majority of things, life chucks your way, along comes a narcissist, and blows everything you've learned out of the water.

The very fact that you have bought or borrowed this book means that a narcissist has somehow managed to get under your skin. So, perhaps already you have dipped a toe in and paid a heavy price.

For simplicity's sake, how about we say there's a narcissistic involvement scale, and it goes 1-10. The lower the number, the lesser your involvement. At this stage, you will have the confidence and trust in your judgment to end the relationship before it gets messy.

Once it gets to the middle numbers, you are at the stage where the narcissist has sussed out your vulnerabilities and capitalized on them. You will be giving them continual benefits of doubt, while in your heart of hearts, you know what you must do. The trouble is, you just cant bring yourself to do it.

By the time you get to the magic number 10, it is game over. Self-confidence, self-belief, and self-esteem—just about everything is well and truly on the floor. However, a long, painful, drawn-out recovery process lies ahead.

Just how could you have been so stupid?

Well, here's how.

To begin with, let's look at how you got off and running with the narcissist. I'll come at this from two angles.

The first is to assume you have had no experience of them in the past and that this is your first time. The second, and more problematic, is based on the repeat pattern of dating narcissists and some potential causes of this, shall we say, repeat offending.

Behavior which, unless it's reined in, will be doing your long-term health no favors, probably through your copious consumption of alcohol, or cigarettes, or maybe something even more potent.

So, here you are, cruising along in life, everything seems to be going your way, more through serious effort and thoughtful decision than by pure chance. But you are still missing that vital someone to share it all with. Wouldn't that be the icing on the cake?

Along comes an as yet unidentified narcissist, and what do you know, they seem to be able to tick a whole load of your ever so hard to please boxes. You try so hard to avoid getting carried away, but hey, what's not to like, and you seem to get on so well.

The script is predictable, and the inevitable follows, those little tests they use to reveal vulnerability clues. You may have the hots, but your no schmuck and certainly don't expect to be treated as one. You'll forgive this the once, but you set the record straight about what will and will not be tolerated in this relationship.

You gauge from the response that this doesn't go down too well, but good for you, as they go back to being all lovey-dovey before starting their minor transgressions all over again.

Nope, sorry, this is not good enough. Too much nonsense too early on, you, with enough relationship experience behind you and the self-confidence to make the hard decisions, you call it a day. No ifs, no buts, no second chances. To be fair, by the second month, the narcissist would probably have known that there were no vulnerabilities in your psyche available for exploitation.

They quickly move on when they know the mileage is limited, but bravo to you for sending them packing first. That would have stung their fragile ego. On the narcissistic involvement scale, you probably never even made a two, and all this without experience.

Good for you. Not all novices get off so lightly, but that's what inner confidence can do. It is the ability to do what everyone knows they SHOULD do. It's just that the doers do it, and the procrastinators don't.

Now, imagine the same coasting along scenario, but this time a significant event that you may or may not have seen coming happens in your life. It could be the loss of a family member or friend, your best friend moving away, or the loss of your job.

Whatever the event, it's enough to impose a temporary loss of confidence, a chink in your otherwise steely coat of armor. Somehow things don't feel the same without someone beside you to prop you up or validate those tough decisions that used to come so quickly.

You have a bit more thinking time on your hands nowadays, whereas things always seemed spontaneous before. Now meeting someone seems ever more attractive. It would be nice to have your spirits raised now that your nights are just that little bit longer.

You have a bit more space to fill, and there are only so many visits to the gym or hobbies you can do without it all seeming a bit monotonous. It would be nice if you could meet someone kind and caring. You will.

It's just that they will be of the chameleon-like—narcissistic—variety. How did they become the kind of person you so wanted to meet? I'll tell you. Because early on, like most human beings, you wanted to share your story and offload your feelings! You tried to let it all out and feel compassion in return. You will get that compassion. Unfortunately, it's from the wrong person, and it isn't real.

Again, it's the same script. Your new partner could not have come along at a better time. Your spirits are lifted just as they had started to flat line. Then the inevitable testing phase kicks in. This time, how is it handled? As decisively as the first scenario? Or is there a bit more leeway, a few more benefits of doubt given.

The narcissist knows [because you told them] about the chink in your armor and sees a potential opportunity. Yes, you are strong, and of independent thought and decisive [usually] but, you also have emotions, which are being played to the hilt.

Your new partner is now off and running, and the pattern will be as discussed several times already. How far you allow yourself to move up the narcissistic involvement scale is entirely down to you. But it will surely be a high number.

There is one final scenario to be included under the umbrella of the narcissistic novice, and that is plain and simple complacency.

The first scenario involved the novice who still had their wits about them. The second involves the novice whose confidence has taken a bit of a hit. In this scenario, I suggest it is the easiest thing in the world to simply drop your guard and become too trusting, the ideal prey for opportunistic predators.

In a nutshell, what I'm suggesting is that you should remain vigilant at all times. Unless your potential suitors are prepared to undergo a lie detector test, I can't see any other way. If there's a one in six chance that a potential partner is a narcissist, would you not go into a relationship with your eyes that bit wider open than if the odds were of lottery winning proportions? Of course, you would.

As for complacency, that adage is as true today as it always was. If someone or something looks too good to be true, it probably is. I suggest that if you are complacent, you run the risk of even greater manipulation because narcissists will see you as nothing more than a soft target.

The chapter entitled 'Red Flags – Does any of this sound familiar?' might prove enlightening for those more trusting souls. The intention is to alert you to some of those 'Uh-ho' alarm bell moments.

Repeat offending? Now, this is where you do owe it to yourself to get a handle on the situation. It does happen in life that some people are plain unlucky. But if you're on your third narcissist, it is safe to say there is more to this than plain bad luck. It will not be easy, but it is within your grasp to change. Because sure as hell your narcissistic partner won't!

Now, I am always prepared to listen to people who have been around the block a few times. It is pretty much irrelevant what they have achieved.

To me, if someone attains something from a standing start, they are worth listening to, for no other reason than their taste of human interaction and experiences will be considerable. The point of this preamble is to recount a saying by Andrew Carnegie which has been stuck in my mind since I read it a decade ago. And it's this:

'The older I get, the more I go by what people do and not what they say!'

Okay, it could have been anyone who said this, and there are countless variations, 'actions speaking louder than words' being the one most often bandied about. However, Carnegie's just seemed to resonate that little bit more. I have no idea if he intended it to apply to relationships, but as the world's richest businessman in 1878, somehow I doubt it.

With age and experience, I'm sure you can imagine how easy it becomes to catch people out. We all make promises we don't follow through on, and occasionally we have great plans that somehow never seem to come to anything. But shit happens, that's allowed.

With romantic partners, there's always a list of requirements, don't you think? Top of that list tends to be kind and caring. Being trustworthy always helps, followed closely by a sense of humor, romantic, hard-working, interesting, etc., etc. If looks are mentioned, it's usually way down the list...

We all know looks are merely superficial, and we would never be so shallow as to admit to falling for someone based on their looks alone. Then, guess what?

Along comes Mr or Mrs. Narcissist, who usually scores very highly in the visually appealing dept and has the charisma and charm alongside to suck you in. There you are, off on that darn treadmill yet again. Why do some people never learn? The answer could lie in codependency.

Codependents suffer from relationship addiction. Rather than taking things slowly and seeing what develops, codependents have a bull-in-a-china-shop approach. There is no hanging around. It's all guns blazing to find a partner, then hang onto them at any cost.

Codependents usually have a poor sense of self-worth and, at times, debilitatingly low self-esteem. The origins are generally childhood neglect or some form of dysfunctional family experience in the past. At the core of this condition is an excessive reliance on other people for approval or a sense of identity.

You can imagine a narcissist positively salivating at the opportunity presented to them on meeting a codependent. As always with codependents, they are very forthcoming and up front with their feelings. The narcissist's antennae are finely tuned to signs of desperation. Yabba dabba doo, they are telling themselves, in an understated kind of way.

So why do codependents choose narcissists ahead of the abundance of non-narcissists out there? On our ever-expanding climate of single souls looking for companionship, surely there must be a non-narcissist out there with an equally cute ass? The answer is, of course, yes, there are non-narcissists out there, many with the requisite firm buttocks to look good in tight jeans. Looking at it pragmatically, the reasons are simple.

A. Narcissists are masters of the great first impression.

B. Narcissists act faster and are equally quick to commit.

C. Non-narcissists take things much more slowly.

Codependents prefer A and B over C.

That's the easy part to explain, and it's true. Look how quick off the mark Chris was with Sarah. The poor woman hardly had time to draw breath. On the other hand, look at how willingly she allowed herself to be drawn inside his spider's web. Was Sarah aware she was a likely codependent? I doubt it. Narcissists always act fast, in part lest someone else is waiting in the wings to steal their catch.

But what makes someone codependent in the first place? And what lies beneath this desperation for a partner at all costs?

Accepting that you are a codependent is the first step on the road to recovery. The following checklist is not exhaustive. The various codependency websites available can fill you in on the various core characteristics, but the following are the main ones. In essence, you will always put the needs of other people above your own. Always! Which leaves you open to potential exploitation. Think the Sarah story all over again.

You tend to fall in love quite quickly.

You are the ultimate people pleaser. You think nothing of spoiling others with gifts and attention but rarely treat yourself.

You are infinitely more accommodating to partners, friends, and work colleagues than they are you.

You have fragile boundaries as to what will and will not be tolerated. As a result, you allow yourself to be let down more than you should.

You are overly generous, and you help too many people, the same people who in a million years would never reciprocate. You prioritize other people's needs over your own.

You are obsessive and ruminate over every detail of the relationship.

You are hyper-critical of yourself.

Have you found yourself nodding in agreement to a few of these? It's as if you have been conditioned just to give, give, and unable to stop even though you seem to be continuously taken to the cleaners.

Delving into a codependents background will always provide clues as to how this has developed. More often than not, the result of being brought up in a dysfunctional family.

In recent years, the term 'dysfunctional family' has been popularized in the mainstream media, but what does it mean? The general description we all adhere to is an environment that involves a whole load of shouting, door slams, and swearing.

Not to forget several visits a week from Social Services, but actually, this is not the case. For many, the public face of dysfunctional families is one of middle-class respectability. As I always do with characteristics, I list the following as representative of the dysfunctional family. They are not listed by the degree of importance, and each is as bad as the other.

Unloving environment

Unsupportive

Seemingly endless internal conflict

Manipulation

Overly harsh discipline and physical punishment

Blaming

Scary and unsafe

Unrealistic demands placed on children

༄

Now I have to bear in mind that this is a book about relationships, not a book on the ramifications of dysfunctional parenting. That's another book in itself. Suffice to say that children brought up in this environment go without their emotional needs being met. It is the difference between going to school with head held high and shoulders back or walking there with head bowed, shoulders slumped, and the feeling of being unloved and insignificant.

The child who comes home has been passed over for the football team or loses his childhood sweetheart to the more confident fellow pupil. The child who needs love, encouragement, and support instead receives apathy or, worse, criticism! Pleas for help fall on deaf ears.

The greater the need of the child, the greater the likelihood of the parent branding the child a pest or a nuisance, weak, devoid of the stiff upper lip other children they mention seem to have. In no uncertain terms, the child will be told that if they continue with this whiney behavior, they may feel the full force of the parental back hand.

Take a moment to think about this. How would you feel if this had happened to you as a child? The net result of parental apathy and emotional neglect is that the child learns to adopt different strategies, patterns of behavior that become ingrained and are then carried forward into adulthood.

This is an excellent time to introduce narcissistic mothers.

There are two ends of the spectrum.

The first is uninterested and apathetic, as discussed above.

The other end of the spectrum is absolute engulfment and control. The mother becomes obsessively involved in the child's life to the extent that the child loses all identity and independence.

The raisin detre is catering to the mother's needs, not the child, so that the child loses any prospect of developing their value systems, self-confidence, or knowledge as to how to set boundaries. The child's achievements become the mother's achievements. The child is loved when they comply with the mother's request and are given the silent treatment or insults when they do not. Control is maintained by manipulation, playing siblings off against each other: guilt [After everything I've done for you] or just plain physical bullying.

So, that's the spectrum, with varying degrees of dysfunctional parenting in between.

Is there a worse end of the spectrum? Well, neither is great, but from personal experience, I would say the closer it gets to maternal narcissism, the worse it gets, but it's a close call.

So, if you haven't figured it out already, what's the outcome of this crappy, controlled upbringing?

As I mentioned earlier, the child adopts a set of strategies to accommodate the lousy parental influence. The top of the list is to become a people pleaser in the extreme. Whatever it takes, as long as it brings the occasional scrap of affection, attention, or, better still, emotional reward. Academic achievement is ideal, as the narcissistic parent can then claim credit for that as well. A job well done!

The downside of this coping behavior is that complying, accommodating, and pleasing can become so ingrained that it is carried forward into adulthood. Furthermore, it makes the narcissist waiting in the wings the ideal partner to feed off the codependent's giving ways.

Think about it.

The neglected and unloved child who has developed a strategy to win parental approval grows up to become this codependent adult, priding themselves on their ability to second guess what other people want and need, usually before they realize it themselves.

The codependent will put themselves out if the net result is some form of gratitude or meaningful approval, fully compliant, accommodating, and happy to continually play second fiddle.

Having become accustomed to receiving mediocre scraps of love in their formative years, you can imagine their enthusiasm flying off the Richter scale if a potential love interest promises much, much more. And we all know how good narcissists are at making promises.

Along comes the narcissistic potential love interest. Charming, witty, probably good-looking, and above all, NICE! When were their parents ever that nice to the young codependent—in-the-making? The initial flattery and attention will get the narcissist off to a flying start, and when the love bombing follows, the codependent will be blown away. Finally, somebody loves them at last.

No wonder they become hooked so quickly. Even when the nonsense starts, the silent treatment, etc., they recognize and are conditioned to this behavior. All they have to do is keep trying that little bit harder to win back the narcissist's approval.

The narcissist is in control and takes center stage. This is always non-negotiable. And the codependent will always be happy to comply. This pattern of behavior has been set in stone for a very long time.

The relationship deteriorates as the narcissist withdraws. They won the testing period and are now bored, but the codependent clings on. They are used to cling on. They have done it their whole lives, which is no different. If they just keep trying that little bit harder, the partner will see sense! It's the only strategy the codependent knows.

CHAPTER 9

NARCISSISTS AND AGING

In the early days of Reality TV, like a lot of people, I would waste endless hours on an evening as some kind of a fly-on-the-wall looking in on the dozen or so people thrown together 24/7, all to provide some kind of insight into the dynamics or frailties of the human condition. Was I enlightened in any way? You must be joking — this was as good a cure for insomnia as you're ever liable to get.

However, one particular moment stuck in my mind and has remained with me since, long before I ever understood anything remotely significant about narcissism.

So when the idea was recently mooted to include a chapter on aging, it was the first thing that sprang to mind. It was just like one of those flashback memories that seem to pop up when a particular song comes on the radio, or you get the whiff of a particular smell—those golden moments come flooding back.

So picture the scene. The setting took place in one of those faux gardens the program's producers like to set up. Big on Fengshui, imitation grass, potted palms, bamboo, reclining sun loungers, jacuzzi [there always has to be a Jacuzzi], and the inevitable mild pan pipe music wistfully playing in the background. All for the benefit of helping contestants relax after a hard day sitting around the house, playing, and chatting.

In the garden, two of the contestants have siphoned off from the rest and are now in the process of getting to know each other a little bit better.

One is a modern-day pop star, good looking girl in her early twenties, of the one-hit-wonder variety, and the other is also from the music business, but this time a male, safe to say getting on a bit having had a string of hits back in the Seventies.

To save their embarrassment and potentially any libel action [narcissists with money do like their lawsuits], I'll christen them Chloe B and Peter Shapiro. Those are the best Seventies pop star names I could come up with being afraid, so if there are any real-life Peter Shapiro's out there, it is not you, okay??

The conversation went something like this.

'So tell me, Peter, what was it you did?'

Eyebrows closing, there is a quick look of disbelief on his face. He wonders if she is taking the mickey. His laugh is just about as fake as the surroundings.

'Ha Ha. okay, I get it.'

'Get what?'

'The joke. That you don't know who I am.'

'I'm sorry, I don't.'

Trying not to look severely pissed off, his mind is now in overdrive. He now puts on the narcissist's favorite trick, displaying false modesty.

'Okay, try this? You'll know who I am now.' Then, he comes out with the opening bars of his biggest hit.

The quizzical look on her face but with complete innocence.

'No, I don't know that one, Peter. When was that a hit?'

'Are you kidding me? It sold millions. In 1975, it was number one for five weeks! It was number one all over Europe as well. I thought you would get that easy peasy!'

'No, sorry Peter, never heard it before...If you write it down, I could ask my mum. If it was 1975, I'm sure my Grandma would have heard of it. She loved music back then.'

Peter's now miffed. Everyone in the music business must know that record.

'Ok, try this one then.' He starts singing opening bars of another hit but, and for good measure, now throws in his signature Seventies dance routine.

'No, never heard that one either. Can you write that one down as well?'

'Are you kidding me? You're winding me up, right?'

'No, I'm not, honest, I'm not.'

As a last-ditch attempt, he tries a few more. Realizing it's a lost cause, he makes an abrupt excuse before heading off in search of a more appreciative audience. Chloe B shakes her head in a kind of 'Thank God he's gone kind of way' before going back to catching up on some more rays.

Knowing full well the fixed camera will be watching her every move, she is well aware that lying provocatively on the sun lounger will do much more for her street cred than talking to some irritating old has been.

As the days passed, it must have become apparent to Peter that he had no chance of becoming a senior diva in this environment, full of attention-seeking wannabees.

So, drama queen to the last, he chooses his moment to storm out of the exit door, before reaching the outer perimeter fence, with security and production crew in hot pursuit. This was his last moment of attention before the salacious tabloids ran with the story the following day.

It was no matter to him that the press vilified him. He has achieved his aim. His name is back up there, temporarily, of course, but he knows for the next twenty-four hours at least, his name will be the subject of many a water cooler discussion.

As I discussed earlier, there is nothing wrong with the Peter's of this world still wanting attention, everything in moderation. But, as with other C-list celebrities appearing on equally banal TV shows, can it not be earned more positively?

There are charitable causes to consider. Setting up some foundation, hell, even a sponsored walk would do. The answer [as if you didn't know by now] is because it's all about them. They could have capitalized on their talent, looks, or good fortune when it came their way.

Instead, they will have taken all the narcissistic liberties under the sun, pushing their luck, blaming others, surrounding themselves with 'yes' people, and generally just pissing everyone off with their over-the-top antics. Employment is fickle at the best of times, but never more than in the world of entertainment. Developing a reputation for being hard to deal with, and it's game over.

Granted, this is the world of show business, where every detail will be milked to death by the media for the story's sake. Still, in every possible way, Peter's behavior typifies the predicament facing the aging narcissist. With looks fading, gravity taking its toll, and charisma becoming a bit stale, the art of the great first impression no longer applies.

Bang goes the opportunity to seduce newcomers to their rapidly depleting inner circle. That's bad enough, but since they have undoubtedly spent their lifetime taking liberties, word of mouth will now operate as a kind of karma, saving any remaining vulnerable souls from exploitation.

The bad news is, they still think they look like George Clooney or his female equivalent. I first read this a decade ago and found it hard to believe, but further first-hand experience has convinced me it's true.

Aging narcissists think they still cut it in the looks dept irrespective of the amount of hair dye and anti-wrinkle cream stock piled in the bathroom cupboard. So it begs the question, does George Clooney think he still looks fantastic? I mean, will he look in the bathroom mirror when he's 75 and think, 'Heh, you know what. Still got it'.

Somehow you suspect not. He seems to spend a massive amount of time on causes that have nothing to do with self-interest and photo opportunities. Somehow, you just kind of know that George is a good guy. I'll bet he's a great team player too. Either that or he's the consummate narcissist. It's all an act, and he has us all fooled.

Oscar Wilde said in Dorian Gray that everything is possible when you have youth and beauty. It is a fact of life that we naturally gravitate to those who have the kind of looks that make the rest of us green with envy [see George Clooney above].

But what do you do if you are a narcissist, and your looks are on the wane? If you are a narcissist in denial, aging is not a problem because you simply refuse to accept that you are getting older. Like a scene from Snow White, replace the wicked stepmother with the aging narcissist.

'Mirror, mirror, on the wall, who is the fairest one of all?'

'You are, hun, you rock.'

For men, that means wearing clothing and frequenting stores more suitable to those in their twenties. As ever, nothing in moderation! The jeans will be just that bit too tight, and the designer shirt would be more suited to someone at least a couple of decades younger.

It is much the same with women. They will roam the aisles looking for products that will keep their skin glowing and wrinkle-free. Then there are the skirts that make you think, 'Oh, come on dear, who are you trying to kid?' There are hair styles somehow out of sync with their aging faces.

Unfortunately, men cannot get away with the same hair dye as women, and it is always a bit too dark, bordering on a kind of black boot polish effect. Does anyone ever say to these people, 'Come on, rein it in, you're pushing your luck thinking you can get away with that?'

No, they don't.

Why?

Because if it is their nearest and dearest, they will know what will happen if they do. Being told to 'act their age' will inevitably lead to a three-week silent treatment. Narcissists only ever surround themselves with those who will 'suck up', so forget about the narcissist having any capacity to absorb home truths. If it's a friend, if that friend dares to criticize, they will be dropped like a hot potato. Narcissists will never accept even well-meaning criticism.

There's always the gym, of course. But there is nothing worse than an aging narcissist turning up with a leotard and Jane Fonda headband and trendy earphones. There is no danger of an aging narcissist wearing a baggy old tee shirt and past-it trainers.

However, they do like mentioning their trainer, and they are more than capable of telling some major porky pies about the time spent each morning on the rowing machine. Anything to create the right impression!

Of course, if they can afford it, there is always the surgical option. As of 2016, the top surgical procedures for men and women in the UK were as follows.

Breast augmentation

Eyelid surgery

Breast reduction

Face/neck lift

Liposuction

Tummy tuck

Nose job

Fat transfer

Ear correction

Brow lift

There were ten straight years of increases, followed by a decrease in 2017. This probably had more to do with economics than lack of demand. The rise in Botox, teeth whitening, tanning, and contouring—all cheaper options, continues its upward trajectory.

Now I had my teeth done a while back. I gave the dentist carte blanche to do everything apart from teeth whitening. Why? Because when the bus driver opened his mouth, I thought, 'Jeez, if I don't do something soon, I'm going to end up like him.' Was this narcissism? I don't think so. Vanity? Well, maybe a little. But I like to think it was more to do with forwarding planning.

Of course, I am not saying that everyone who gets a surgical procedure or teeth whitened is a raving narcissist. But I am saying that I believe narcissism is on the increase. Do I think narcissists would go under the knife if it kept Mother Nature at bay? Darn, right, I do. Do I believe that social media fuels narcissism? Yes, again, and I'll be covering that same topic in another chapter shortly.

In relationships and still thinking they are God's gift, the aging narcissist will believe themselves attractive to younger romantic partners. This often leads to exploitation if the younger partner sees mileage for financial gain.

Think back to Chris cheating on Sarah with Claire. It was not enough to cheat with someone of his own or Sarah's age—it had to be someone younger and 'fit'. On the face of it, he had all the trappings—the flash car, designer clothes, and no doubt he talked up his job. In a way, he got off lightly. If he had any money, she might have taken him to the cleaners. See chapter 'Can narcissists be out-narcissised?'

If it were just about looks, we'd probably all still make allowances. We all have friends who seem to take aging badly. That does not make them narcissists. But if they are narcissistic, it means they will wake up one day to a basket of consequences. It is bad enough that biology is their enemy.

But the stress of being a narcissist in itself tends to age the body prematurely. All those nasty, bitter endings, whether it be in relationships or employment, take their toll. And what about all the money forked out over the years, maintaining that lifestyle and image? Where does it come from, now that time is running out?

There is no danger of them being sensible and stashing a bit away each month for a rainy day. No wonder many now have to work until they drop, or else hang on like grim death to that long-suffering partner, who really should have left a long time ago. They are now both in a position where, realistically, neither can leave the other. So they slug it out, hating and resenting each other and every minute of their time together.

What does that do for stress levels when the body is creaking as it is? So, aging narcissists tend to be poor, which doesn't help them at all. They cannot afford the flash car or designer clothes anymore. To a normal person, that's not great, but it's life. Shit happens! To a narcissist, however, it's an absolute disaster.

You can only churn out the same old lines and the same old charm offensive for so long before everyone finally wakes up. And when they do, the narcissist's former friends and acquaintances will avoid them rather than feeling sympathy for them.

The phone will no longer ring, and the invitations will have dried up. They made no effort, quite the contrary, so why should any effort be made for them? Everyone will be more guarded and less gullible than before.

Word of mouth will spread and will validate what everyone already suspected. This person is not to be trusted. So, at the same time, when the narcissist needs attention more, they receive less and less.

For those hanging on to their jobs they can expect no more favors from their employer. They have pushed their luck too many times, so now the employer wants a shot of them as soon as possible, with as few benefits as possible. There will be those in HR thinking, 'Right, now it's payback time.' Results matter more than ever, as the charm is insufficient to make up deficiencies.

That's bad enough, but there will probably be a younger, fitter, better-looking rival working their way up through the ranks. It is survival of the fittest now, and the younger rival will be seen as fresh and bright, compared to the tired old dinosaur who keeps on trotting out the same old lines.

Tantrums increase in frequency and volume. Letters of complaint fly off to all, and sundry, and mountains are made out of molehills.

Normal people tend to mellow with age. Not so the narcissist. They become more bitter because of their circumstance. Attention-seeking becomes more extreme.

For the aging narcissist, it is a case of the game being up. They have no one to blame but themselves. They promised so much but delivered so little. Everyone they pissed off on the way is now ignoring them.

Interestingly, if a narcissist has scarred you, you are never neutral about them. You will never call them after a few years for a catch-up drink. You have nothing to do with them. So, the aging narcissist has a problem. Their social circle is small to non-existent. They receive no calls or visits. For someone who thrives off attention, this is terrible.

What happens, in the end, is that the narcissist gets a taste of their own medicine. First, they never cared about anyone else, and now no one cares about them.

Remember the 'Aging Roadie' I mentioned a few chapters back? The one who ticks every box for 'If I were chocolate, I would eat myself' criteria! Well, there he was again, last Sunday. Queue a mile long at the solitary till in operation at the local supermarket, and guess who was holding everyone up with their theatrical complaining?

CHAPTER 10

CAN NARCISSISTS BE 'OUT-NARCISSISED'?

Have you ever heard of Assortive mating? Neither had I, until doing some background work into a topic that's been niggling away at the back of my mind for the past year or so. You know how the same thing keeps happens again and again, and you wonder why? There's usually a pattern in there somewhere...

So how did the question of narcissists being out narcissised come about?

I have to go back to my unfortunate experience with a glamorous female narcissist, who was my induction into the subject in the first place. Well, and truly taken to the cleaners but still kept plugging away, telling myself that if I kept trying that little bit harder, she would come to her senses and come crawling back begging for forgiveness.

If only I knew then what I know now.

That's the dreary part. What makes it more interesting is sometime later, when she became involved in a relationship where the roles were entirely reversed, and this time it was her on the receiving end.

How do I know this? Because sometimes even narcissists need a shoulder to cry on, and even though she must have regretted it later, she did divulge enough detail for me to play amateur detective.

The easy part was his Facebook profile. Talk about ticking every box in the last chapter. There were selfies by the bucketload, clearly airbrushed, the odd several hundred or so friends, and endless postings centered around, you guessed it, himself.

That's the attention taken care of. Throw in a hefty dose of control, with a liberal sprinkling of blowing hot and cold with her, and you have all the hallmarks of a complete narcissistic pro.

How was this even possible? How could someone who had these same said characteristics be so out-manipulated by someone behaving identically? As the Queen famously said to the phenomenally well-paid bright spark's who worked in the City after the 2008 financial crash. 'Why did you not see this coming?'

I even thought it might be a double bluff at one stage, but boy, I got that one completely wrong. If you could call it that, this relationship played out entirely to the script going through all the phases mentioned above until the inevitable happened, and it went KAPUT. She came a cropper, and at one point, I nearly felt sorry. But, to be fair, I think the feeling lasted no more than six seconds.

Where the intrigue developed further was in her personal history. She was dumped by her husband of some twenty-odd years for a younger version of herself. She once described a man as having all the attributes of her current flame, so here she was, at it all over again and once more on the receiving end.

There had been several others between the pair, where she was in control, where I was but one of many unfortunate victims. But, in reality, nothing more than a distraction! How do I know this? Because she told me! Narcissists do like to brag about popularity.

She could have been lying, but given her looks, she would not have been short of male interest, and everything she said ties subsequently in with a narcissist's need for attention and inability to survive on their own without some form of companionship.

Was she now conditioned to dating narcissists because of her long-term marriage, or was it like attracting like? I thought it might be the first point. I had not even remotely considered the second.

So which is it?

The principle of Assortive mating proposes that like really does attract like, and that similarity in basic qualities will lead people to bond with each other. The evidence for this is fairly well established.

Humans mate assertively according to age, IQ, height, weight, nationality, education, occupation, and personality. I thought this must be wrong regarding look, as I always sought out the most attractive partner. The studies suggest not. We tend to go for someone as attractive as us. Billionaires and Oligarchs can occasionally be exceptions to this rule.

This is all perfectly plausible, but what happens when you throw narcissism into the equation? Can two exploitative, anti-social, and manipulative people seek out then cling to their soul mate? Can Bonnie meet Clyde and have a relationship of any longevity?

It appears they can start relationships and will, indeed, be attracted to each other. But as to the longevity, that's a whole different story.

Let's start with them getting together in the first place.

Narcissists may be self-important, manipulative, selfish, and greedy, but they can fall in love just as easily as the rest of us. Since they love being in love, maybe even more so. In the early days, will each narcissist be aware of the mask the other is wearing?

Not a chance. Remember, this is the Idealisation phase, where both partners are on their best behavior, each believing the other is 'the one'. As the honeymoon draws to a close, both partners now begin to reveal their true colors. A testing period will start, and how the other reacts determines the path this relationship will take.

Again, this is no different fr4om what would happen if there was only one narcissist in the pair. Since neither party will have been blessed with even a modicum of self-awareness, the other's behavior will be seen as unfair, but the reality is that both parties are now jockeying for position. It becomes a question of who blinks first, in essence, which of them loves the other the most.

Although narcissists are often seen as larger-than-life characters, this is not always the case.

There are two types. Grandiose and Vulnerable! Grandiose is the more in-your-face of the two. They feel superior and have very high self-esteem, their parents having praised them to the hilt from a very early age.

They do not care how their partner views them and may just walk away from the relationship if they do not deserve the praise and admiration. This is the type that will have multiple relationships/affairs. They can be very aggressive when they don't get what they want.

Vulnerable narcissists, as the name suggests, tend to be more emotionally sensitive. They feel anxious or victimized when not treated like royalty and live in perpetual fear of abandonment or rejection. This probably dates back to childhood trauma. They swing back and forth between feeling superior and inferior, depending on what's happening in their lives.

Now one swallow does not a summer make, and my three examples will hardly have the academic fraternity quaking in their boots. But I believe the difference in narcissistic types explains why some narcissistic relationships go one way and others. But I firmly believe that 'love' is involved in all three, and it just so happened that the men were Grandiose narcissists and the woman was Vulnerable.

Let's go back to the first of my examples, the femme fatale. As narcissists cannot stand being on their own for any length of time, my role fulfilled three of her pressing needs: a distraction, a sounding board, and company.

As a narcissist of the more Vulnerable variety, the loss of her grandiose partner of some twenty years standing must have crushed her. Yet, she was still in awe of him.

I remember her telling me that the minute he walked into a room, he took center stage. Even though she was a narcissist with great looks, she envied aspects of his character. For example, his self-confidence and his ability to make a great first impression.

Narcissists are an envious breed in general, so one narcissist can still feel in awe of another. Do I think he was a grandiose narcissist? For sure! Readily admitting that she suspected many infidelities and that major decisions in the marriage were all made by him. Yet, she was still in love with him. Where would she now get those attributes that she lacked herself but wanted so much? He had upped sticks and gone.

She had three months of distraction with me, a few afterward with others, and now she was at it all over again. Then a narcissist of the Grandiose type came along, and she fell hook, line, and proverbial sinker for him.

In an assortive way, they were well matched. He was as good-looking as her. Here she was, playing second fiddle yet again but in a way, by now, conditioned to her predicament. He ran rings round her, to my amusement. Talk about reaping what you sow!

So, what were his attributes, and was it now the case that narcissists only get out-narcissised when they see in others what they wish they had themselves? Sadly, I will never know and can only hazard a cynical guess. Either she would cut her losses before history repeated herself, or else he could make the decision for her.

The second of the two examples is a good-looking woman, early forties. Have known her a few years, and she is your archetypal social media fanatic. She is a lovely person but utterly unreliable with a few husbands, and god knows how many jobs are already under her belt. Mildly self-aware for a narcissist, a rare disposition indeed!

Although her frantic lifestyle appears to be catching up, there has still been no end of men wishing they could be the one but, she does have this nasty habit of getting involved with the narcissistic womanizing variety. Her last partner had the worst possible reputation going for being unfaithful, but off she went and fell head over heels, coming a cropper in the process.

Her friends warned her as, let's face it, word eventually gets round. But no, this time, he said she would change him. Shock, horror, the inevitable happened, and that fragile heart of hers took another beating. The new partner with whom she now lives is, unfortunately, heading in a similar direction.

From the first year of each professing undying love on social media, it's now been left to her to try and keep things afloat. She readily admits he's the one that wears the trousers in that household. Leaving him is non-negotiable, plus the bottom line is she has no place else to go having burned all her bridges and moved in with him a while back.

She tells me he regularly taunts her with threats of eviction, knowing full well her only source of refuge after that would be a woman's shelter, as funds are non-existent. To say her confidence is on the floor would be an understatement. One of these days, I am expecting a late-night knock on the door.

The third example involves a couple. Well, a couple of narcissists actually who also happen to be married. For the benefit of discretion and to ease the storyline, let's call them Ted & Liz. I got to know Ted a good decade ago through work, so it was kind of around the same time that I met femme fatale in Glasgow.

Inevitable that events in such proximity were always going to leave their mark. Anyway, back to the story with Ted. I met Ted through work, and straight away, there was a rapport.

We both came from the same area, shared similar humor, and to be honest, Ted made me feel good as he was just so damn charismatic. He was tall, well I am tall, but he carried his height much better, and he had a bit of an aura. Great start, but only much later on did I learn the hard way, along with quite a few others, that he's a complete bullshitter and absolute chancer.

But in the early days, driving into work knowing that Ted was there made the journey on a wet miserable January less onerous. Me and Ted just got on so well. [Think back to chapter Narcissists as friends] Invites over to his place on a Friday night to share a Chinese takeaway only bolstered his image that here's someone who's done alright for themselves. Large farmhouse out in the country, couple of acres of land, and the Porsche parked up outside the front door. It would be red, of course, with personalized plates for kudos.

As time passed, it was apparent Ted reveled in his success and did appear to love himself a bit more than most, as did his wife, Liz. The script played out identically to my chapter on narcissists as friends, and, as I saw Ted at work most days, it was apparent he could also be a bit of a ladies' man as he confessed to the occasional infidelity on more than one occasion.

Unlike most friendships of this variety, this one ended abruptly, though, and I remember it well. Two years into the friendship, I dared to criticize Ted on an evening during dinner. Not in a heated way, but I was not for backing down.

The next day, I received a phone call from Ted that told me Liz did not want me back in their house in no uncertain terms. This is after a multitude of favors and no end of lending items, some of the value, which was never returned or, if they were, usually in poorer condition than they had been.

Ted sometime later was sacked from his job for fiddling his mileage allowances, and I subsequently discovered he did have previous when it came to pushing his luck. His antics bore all the hallmarks of my chapter on narcissists in the workplace. It transpired that the image the pair of them manufactured of material success was also a sham—rented house, leased car, propensity to move and change jobs regularly.

Were the pair of them as bad as each other? I guessed so, but still, for all Ted's infidelities and erratic lifestyle Liz would never hear a bad word against and woe betide anyone who dared say so.

She was as bad as him in several areas, such as charm and manipulation, but I concluded he was the top dog on balance. Was this another instance of a narcissist being out narcissised? I always thought that narcissists had to be Number one irrespective of partner but now clearly not.

These three examples do not make a conclusive theory but enough to think there may be some mileage to be had. Assortive mating has not done anything to dissuade me that narcissists really can meet their match.

So I have concluded that those high in narcissism can become and stay a couple. However, it comes with conditions, and there is a clear pecking order. As long as the more Vulnerable of the two sees in their more grandiose partner some of the attributes they lack, the grandiose one will always be able to out-narcissise their vulnerable counterpart.

That's relationships taken care of. But what about the question of being out narcissised in friendships or the workplace? Can that happen too, and my answer is a resounding 'Yes'!

It is a question of the hierarchy. We always know someone who has more than us. Whether material possessions, status, or title, most of us just say 'that's life' and move on. We have other more important things to worry about. But narcissists are a different breed. They are never happy with what they have and aspire to bigger and better things. In layman's terms, this is known as 'sucking up'.

The narcissist who has it all will be on the receiving end of this and will love it. The sucker upper will do a brilliant job, gushing out praise at every opportunity in the hope that the party invitations keep rolling in.

The inferior narcissist is only there to make up the numbers and provide free entertainment, but for sure, they will always put on a great show. This is in case the guest invites eventually dry up, which they invariably do.

The worst part of this from the inferior narcissist's perspective is that they have to spend the best part of the night talking about someone else and feeding someone else's ego.

This is instead of others feeding their own, although hopefully someone there of lower hierarchy to replenish their ego at some point. Try and imagine how grating it is for them to return home on an evening from a night out with virtually no plaudits or back slaps to brag about.

So what about workplace out-narcissisation? [Oxford English Dictionary eats your heart out.

Imagine the narcissistic manager who wants to move up the pecking order. They will follow instructions from a narcissistic superior, no matter how ludicrous those instructions may be.

They will socialize with this superior at every available opportunity, and if that means them missing out on family life, so be it. They will praise the superior endlessly but prepare to be the company whipping boy should circumstances dictate. They will occasionally be set up as the fall guy if things go wrong. They will be left to pick up the pieces on their own should that happen.

This person is a total 'Yes-man'. But in turn, they will have their own 'yes-men' underneath to stroke their ego as required.

You must know how it works by now!

CHAPTER 11

NARCISSISTS AND SOCIAL MEDIA

Here I go again, banging on about everything in moderation. Now I'm going to apply it to Social Media.

How many of us on the wrong end of a narcissistic relationship or friendship still troll these same said ex acquaintances in the hope that their ridiculousness or capacity for blatant lying will validate our decision to terminate as being the right one?

Through their online antics, we are never left disappointed. Why is this? Because with social media, there are no boundaries. Not that your average narcissist respects these at the best of times, but with a free reign to do and say as they please, the Genie well and truly really does come out of the bottle.

My point earlier cited social media as a contributing influence behind the inevitable rise in narcissism over the past decade. No small amount of research was carried out on the subject by those infinitely more qualified and better paid than I, and just about all the results are available to view online.

Given that academics do have this nasty habit of devoting several years to a subject only to end up stating what we all kind of knew already, the majority of studies do not disappoint.

Self-promotion has become the order of the day, so much so that the leader of the free world has now gotten in on the act, with his almost obsessive daily feeds on Twitter. When things happen to this extent, you know that things are changing out there in the big wide world. If it's good enough for him...!

On the other hand, is it a prerequisite that narcissism will naturally follow suit as aging economies mature and with an accompanying increase in living standards? Is the apparent rise applicable to only Western culture, or have the underdeveloped nations seen their inhabitants get a bit, well you know, up themselves alongside our own, even without Facebook, Snapchat, or Instagram propelling things along nicely.

Somehow I doubt it, but if anyone wants to fund me while I take 3 yrs out traveling to the few remotest places the planet has left to offer, then, as always, drop me a line. I don't doubt for one minute that social media is a significant influence behind this narcissistic epidemic, as some academics now call it. Indeed, some in the US liken the upward trajectory of narcissism to that matching obesity levels. Now that is scary.

What is crystal clear is that for tens of millions of people across the globe, checking your 'status' first thing in the morning has now become as much of the same daily routine as reaching out for the early morning cup of coffee.

Not that I belong in that category, but, for sure, I am a frequent user. If my friends on Facebook are anything to go by [all 22 of them], then it looks as if we all post the same kind of things.

There are obligatory holiday snaps with the kids, the odd rant, witty sketch, new dog photos, and nights out. You get the gist.

In essence, we have almost always done a twenty-first-century rehash of things anyway, but this time all kind of under the one umbrella and, of course, quicker, and so much more convenient. This is the only social media site I use.

I guess in the main because it was the first that came along, so there's the familiarity element, and also because I like a bit of dialogue alongside. It also appears to be a bit of a generational thing with the more mature amongst us using Facebook while the younger fraternity opts for either Instagram or Twitter. On the other hand, Narcissists can use all three—the more outlets for self-expression, the better.

So as a regular Joe, how do I differ from narcissists using social media? In short, very little. It's not that we are not doing the same things. All of us want to be represented in a way that is hopefully appealing to others.

But for a narcissist, this can never be enough. My point about everything in moderation yet again. Social media represents their real opportunity to shine, to stand out from the crowd, and be seen in the best light possible. In essence, their very own attention-seeking Theatre of Dreams!

No impulse seat of the pants postings from them. Everything has to be carefully thought through and rehearsed, rehearsed and rehearsed again before the adoring audience gets their chance to see the post.

As narcissists have a grandiose inflated self-image, they are addicted to social media endorsements such as 'likes', 'shares', or simply winning new friends. The majority of whom they will never have even heard of before, let alone met. But with distant, superficial connections, there is less opportunity to be found out, and that suits them fine.

Smoke and mirrors really can become the order of the day. If you suspect a friend or partner may already be a narcissist, then social media really should just be the icing on the cake. Here's what gives them away.

PHOTOGRAPHS

Always the first example that springs to mind, and they always display the telltale signs. No danger of the narcissist having a 'that'll do' approach to pictures. Heaven forbid those holiday snaps being reduced to just standing there on the beach holding hands and breathing in at the appropriate moment lest it all hang out. No, no, no, this is their opportunity to give 'Hello' magazine a run for its money.

Everything seems that bit too contrived with pictures taken that were anything but spontaneous. For sure, 'Selfies' have become the order of the day, and boy, we all know how much narcissists love their 'selfies' nowadays.

Not all selfie-takers are narcissists, though. This is important because assuming that this represents the defining criteria on social media is to miss the point and allow the real deal of fully-fledged narcissists to slip under the radar.

Either way, I still categorize the genuine narcissistic selfie enthusiasts as the more amateur of the species. The real deal narcissists go way beyond buying themselves a selfie stick and prefer the more Hollywood approach, albeit on the cheap.

Those side-angle shots, or how about thoughtful or contemplative? The James Dean mean and moody look seems to be gaining prominence amongst men, and have you noticed how many black & white pics seem to be becoming 'de rigeur'.

They must spend a fortune on the best cameras because the picture quality is always of a very high standard. Think 'Hello' magazine again and also my references to the running cost of being a narcissistic club member.

Ultimately, for men, no matter the age, clothing will always be a worm that enhances their social status. Don't be surprised to see designer shades being worn out of season. As long as they think it makes them look like something out of a Ridley Scott movie, so be it.

Much the same with women. Clothing and makeup only enhance their attractiveness and a bit more cleavage or leg than you would otherwise expect. Either way, in both cases, what the photographs will show is the degree of preparation beforehand.

Those impulse shots took a whole load longer than they are prepared to admit, and heaven help their long-suffering poor partner roped in as an assistant. This is a one-way street. Photographs will be selected with the due care and attention given to Fleet Street Editorials finest.

For group photographs where there is not quite the same degree of control or freedom for expression, still, the opportunity nonetheless to be center stage. If a group, watch who's standing in the middle. If everyone's seated around the large table, watch to see who raises their glass the highest or decides to stand just as the button hits 'click'.

See who chooses to sit on someone's knee to grab the limelight or crawl between another's legs. Watch to see who appears to be laughing or singing the loudest. Whatever it takes, they have to stand out from the crowd.

Think back to the storyline with Chris and Sarah attending the party. Always the life and soul whenever the sniff of a photo opportunity came along and making damned sure he's center stage with Sarah, who by this time knows the ropes, his willing stooge alongside.

Such was his bravado. He even has the audacity to have some photos retaken. Bet your bottom dollar next morning before breakfast he's online to check his number of 'likes'. Woe betide if Sarah was not one of them.

These are what I call the real deal narcissists, clever, well not that clever actually, but intelligent enough to go about getting attention in a less obvious but for sure much more manipulative way.

Now just to backtrack to the Selfie fraternity for a moment and pick up on my point about some of them being unnecessarily branded as narcissists. Given that the word 'Selfie' itself has now entered the Oxford English Dictionary, let me enlighten you with the results of several recent studies, effectively singing from the same sheet as they frequently do and pigeonholing selfie-takers into three categories.

First, there are the Communicators. Photos taken with the primary intention of engaging fellow social media friends in dialogue. There is nothing up with this. If the selfie manages to include a bit of backdrop and is of sufficient interest, then where's the harm? Truth be told, I quite like these ones and will usually respond.

Next come the Autobiographers, recording critical moments in their lives for posterity. For this, I read as an updated equivalent of the old Family album. Again, am ok with that.

Finally, and apparently, this was the smallest of the group's, come the self-publicists. The narcissists, in other words, posting anything and everything in return for being seen in a better light. Don't be surprised to see the resulting pictures airbrushed or enhanced for this batch before being released to a broader viewing audience—no danger of many backdrops with this variety.

In fact, with so much of their face on the show, the picture could, for all intents and purposes, have been taken anywhere. These are the kind of pictures that show the disparity between how they appear online and how they tend to look in the flesh.

The type of picture that makes you think, 'Oh for god's sake, who are you trying to kid' irrespective of the intention to maintain the identity of being superior and desirable. Do you think Chris was the type to airbrush his pictures, or is the Pope not a Catholic after all?

POSTINGS

All designed, of course, to bring attention upon themselves, the common thread running through all preceding chapters, the extent of which is measured by the amount of positive feedback or 'likes'.

Unfortunately for narcissists, the Law of Diminishing returns is as applicable to Facebook postings as it is in economic theory. Explained as 'the point at which the level of profits or benefits gained is less than the amount of money or energy invested'. In this instance, put simply, people just get fed up.

It never ceases to amaze me just how quickly people can tire of something that was once the thing to do and when faced with someone who seems infatuated with showing the world just how gorgeous they are, well, in the end, it just becomes a bit predictable and a tad embarrassing.

Where the 'likes' were once on double figures with the narcissist on cloud nine, things will eventually slow down to just a trickle with the narcissist facing the dilemma of becoming ever more extreme or simply seeking new friends to keep the feedback rolling in. Guess what? Never one for half measures. They do both.

Deficiencies of narcissistic supply just mean upping the ante with online posts. Pictures are just half of it, albeit the preferred option.

But there are also telling the world what seems to be happening in your life at this present moment in time. Polar opposites with elation on the one hand and some good melodrama on the other but at least guaranteed to elicit some short-term feedback.

When sharing news, I always think there's an etiquette to adopt, and you won't be surprised to hear me mention the word moderation. Unless friends happen to be of the very long term through thick and thin variety personal news will be shared in general terms without getting into the specifics.

Not so with narcissists. With attention on the wane in order to keep up the momentum, the kind of information shared will be that of the best kept to yourself variety. If you're familiar with the adage 'Washing your dirty linen in public,' you'll know what I mean by this.

Another significant clue is in the writing style. Do they use 'I', 'Me', or 'My' a lot? Do they swear in their posts? Unsurprisingly, narcissists tend to speak more about themselves, and funny how when describing a problem or situation, it always seems to be them that saves the day.

FRIENDS

Think back to the previous chapter, 'Narcissists and attention.' The way narcissists need people is the same way the rest of us need oxygen to survive. When social media came along, they must have thought all their Xmas's had come at once. Winning friends with the most minuscule of effort, how utopian is that for a narcissist?

All they have to do in the 'real' world is keep meeting people, albeit in a distant, shallow way, which is what they do anyway. Stick in a friend request and 'Heh presto' another trophy, another follower, and another sucker to share your likes and dislikes until the inevitable happens and they tire of the persona bearing tiny semblance to reality!

The thing with Facebook and the like is that most of us never actually hit the unfriend button very often. When we tire of someone, we simply tend to ignore, so for the narcissist, the number keeps merely growing alongside their ego irrespective of the fact the majority simply no longer care. It is a case of quantity over quality.

However, for those who want 'unfriended,' here are a few simple pointers that guaranteed success or your money back.

1. Criticize in public. You will be dropped like a brick.

2. Imply on a posting that they do not know what they are talking about. Again, much the same impact as above, but at

least you have the fun of knowing all their latest friends will have read the post as well.

3. Make a fool of their photos. Not only will you be dumped, but seething resentment held against you for the rest of their lives.

On the other hand, you may just want to remain friends, sit back and enjoy the free entertainment on offer. As for me, I just enjoy winding them up too much to be afforded the luxury.

CHAPTER 12

FIFTY STAGES TO DATING A NARCISSIST!

The following order may vary one or two points here and there, but, generally speaking, this is the format. Of course, you may already be on the ladder, in which case try and pinpoint exactly where you are on the scale in anticipation of what is yet to follow.

1. Great first impression. Bowled over by a combination of looks, charm, wit, and charisma. Would you like to see this person again? You bet!

2. First date. There appears to be a mutual rapport, and they are so easy to talk to. You have lots in common, and their interests mirror yours.

3. The first night together. Sure there is lust, but also a whole load more.

4. The love bombing begins. Endless texts, phone calls, and nights out. You both seem unable to get enough of each other.

5. The first weekend away. Time to yourselves. Get to know each other better. Their relationship history is much more complicated than yours: several bitter endings and estranged family. Hell, no one is perfect.

6. They love showing you off to friends and particularly on social media. No shortage of pictures or messages of undying love.

7. Spending so much time in each others company the idea is mooted of living together.

8. You notice they seem to like the limelight and can be impatient. Again you forgive.

9. Now thinking of them 24/7 this time does feel different. Not gone unnoticed, the discernible spring in your step.

10. Friends comment on how well you seem to be suited.

11. Your family approves and is equally enthusiastic.

12. You know you are in love. It's mutual because they told you so. No one has ever made them feel the way you do. They are the first to come out with the term 'soul mate'.

13. Occasional criticism of appearance or habits. They can be volatile. A bathroom towel left on the floor or milk in the fridge without its lid can be all it takes to set them off in a rage.

14. Often moody, you wonder if now out of favor. No reassurance on offer. Simply told you overthink things.

15. Phone calls and texts slow down to a crawl. After several months you tell yourself this is only to be expected.

16. Weekends away are a thing of the past. Nights out now consist of meeting their friends or indulging in their hobbies.

17. Now aware of a selfish streak, it's time you pointed it out. This does not go down well. No argument but simply silence, which lasts.

18. They blow hot and cold. You are now continually walking on eggshells.

19. Days can go by with no contact. Are they seeing someone else?

20. Friends voice concern. It transpires this person has a bit of a reputation.

21. They reestablish contact. Lot on their minds, so they had to take time out. You are told not to worry but maybe should cool things off a bit. You are perplexed by the sudden contradiction.

22. You feel rejected and become desperate. This relationship is everything to you. You have become needy and hate yourself for it in the process.

23. They have gone AWOL, but it's now you that's climbing the wall in despair. Why do they keep doing this to you?

24. Once again, they reestablish contact but this time no excuses. Up to you now to do all the running.

25. Halfway through the Top 50, and this is the point of no return. Lick your wounds or prepare to sell your soul.

26. You stayed in, and now they have total control. You relinquished yours at No 25.

27. Criticism now occurs regularly. Most of it is personal and hurtful.

28. Doubting yourself becomes standard. Self-esteem is falling to the floor.

29. Being given treats becomes a thing of the past.

30. Your friends have long gone. They gave up on your partner, having seen the warning signs long ago.

31. Goaded at home and criticized in public, arguments between you become commonplace.

32. Drink and/or cigarettes now fill a void with increasing regularity.

33. Your partner is now openly flirtatious. You suspect an affair. Bedroom activity is on the wane.

34. They become evasive and secretive. They claim to be working harder than usual.

35. You find yourself playing detective more and more.

36. They seem to be adding more friends on social media. You know none of these people.

37. You are now certain of their infidelity and confront. You are accused of paranoia.

38. They appear more agitated than usual. Financial misgivings come to light. Your help is sought. You will, of course, be repaid. Unusual behavior blamed on external pressures

39. Back on good behavior but short-lived. Their infidelity uncovered. They claim a one-off, passing the buck in your direction.

40. You forgive but let it be known it will not be tolerated.

41. The offense is recommitted shortly thereafter but with a different partner. Time for you to walk.

42. They plead. Every excuse under the sun, but this time falling on deaf ears.

43. You leave but are still hounded to reconsider.

44. Midnight phone calls and begging letters before they turn nasty.

45. You establish a firm policy of no contact.

46. They now follow and stalk. A smear campaign ensues. Your immediate family is contacted, as are your friends.

47. Watch out for accusations on social media. Their new partner is flaunted for the whole world to see.

48. The penny drops 12 months later, just how big a mug you have been.

49. The current partner is now making contact with the same concerns as yours from the past. You notice the identical script.

50. You familiarize yourself with patterns of narcissistic behavior. From now on, you will establish clear boundaries which will never be crossed. You live a happier life as a result.

CHAPTER 13

THE NARCISSIST IN YOUR WORKPLACE

Incredible from my perspective how just one person can make such a difference. Just one, that's all it takes, just one.

The sports pages make great play of the about-turn a team experiences when a new coach is appointed. There are a few changes here and there, and before you know it, the squad has galvanized, and off they go on a winning run.

Look at the stock market. It just loves it when an underperforming company appoints a new CEO, and twelve months later, what do you know, sales are up, losses are stemmed, margins improve, and all becomes well again with that once flagging share price.

I've always been useless at sports and was never destined to experience life as a power broker but having worked at the coal face on many an occasion, I think I can speak with some authority in the one defining quality the best managers seem to have, and that's an uncanny ability at identifying the narcissistic prima donnas bringing their business or team down and getting shot of them ASAP.

How many times have you had that feeling when you go to work? You know how it is, the minute you walk through the main doors you just 'feel it', the atmosphere, hard to explain what it feels like exactly but it's not great, is it? The kind of atmosphere that makes the time pass a whole load slower than it would typically do.

It makes no difference that you cannot see the cause of the atmosphere because you know they are there, somewhere, and you know by now that everyone else on the same shift probably feels the same.

It matters little if a factory unit containing hundreds or an office floor with just a handful of people, all it takes is just that one person to make what's left of the day feels that bit grimmer.

Not like that in the beginning, though, never is. Here's a fresh face come on the scene. Charismatic, bubbly, always got the right line at the right time and seems to have that annoying habit of being liked by everyone, that is, until the Genie comes out of the bottle.

Working with a narcissist within a contained environment for 8-10 hours a day, five days a week can be a genuinely dismal experience. Those poor guys who had to work with Maureeeece cramped like sardines down the bowels of the engine room for six months at a time on 12-hour shifts suffering his attention-seeking theatrics, no wonder they all drank like a fish on their time off.

Understanding how they create such lousy environments, you need to go right back to the very beginning, looking no further than the day your Human Resources Manager thought to themselves, 'Oh my, this person looks promising', and for what ensues just note the similarity to early doors relationships. As I keep repeating, no matter the environment, the script remains the same. Always!

The hard part is getting a foot in the door in the first place, of course, and it's at this stage that the narcissists are usually two steps in front of everyone else, sealing the deal with their mastery of the art of the great first impression and think about it? What a great attribute to have in today's ferociously competitive here today gone tomorrow jobs market where secure employment is pretty thin on the ground.

When it's a close-run thing with two or three recruits in the running, the likeability factor will always be the one that sways the decision in their favor, unless, of course, the interviewer is adept at spotting that select band of people who continually walk around with a giant red arrow above their head pointing downwards screaming 'WARNING'.

Not that I want to do the Human Resources world a complete disservice. Interviewers do what they have to do, probing and picking up on a candidate's potential weak points depending on the skill levels required for each job on offer.

However, just as we all raise our game with company research, product knowledge, or just plain selling ourselves, narcissists go a that significant bit further upping the charisma ante.

It usually works a treat unless, of course, the arrogance and attitude have revealed themselves prematurely or the interviewer has the unfortunate experience to draw on and delves that little bit further. Once bitten twice shy as they say.

Assuming the foot is now successfully through the door, things will only continue to get better in the short term as Human Resources gauge positive feedback from the shop floor. A model employee is in the making, but this is the honeymoon period, and you would expect nothing less considering still under probation. Exemplary timekeeper, good team player, and highly productive. But all the while keeping a mindful eye on their fellow employees' character traits.

Who stands out as amenable, who are the nice ones and what's their personal situation, which ones do the most moaning, which ones like attention, where are the quiet ones? In essence, who can be manipulated and brought onside? Never shy away from out of hours socializing.

This is where narcissists can rise to the occasion, becoming the center of attention with humor and charisma. Where better to garner supply with their more vulnerable people-pleasing counterparts.

Narcissists have no empathy, regarding their fellow employees as tools for manipulation or exploitation by adulation, affirmation, or just plain nicking their best ideas, then taking the credit as if their own.

Underneath this promising façade, however, lies an entirely different creature. Inherent feelings of superiority make them highly envious of those in more promising positions and resentful of being reduced to working with colleagues deemed as woefully inferior.

With probation complete, off comes the mask and time for the narcissist to enact their superior skill set. The testing phase begins. [Ring any bells?]

It may only be minor, but the odd five or ten minutes late back from lunch indicates management intent. No action was taken then the door can continue to be prised open that little bit further.

No harm, of course, in passing the odd comment to those in authority about others' non-appearance from work breaks. Of course, only with the company's best interest at heart.

'Oh, I thought they would have been back long ago by now. Don't tell me they are still in the canteen.'

Complaining now moves up a few gears. The shift patterns seem unfair, not that they are making a song and dance about it, of course. Can allowances be made to do specific shifts more than others, as seems to be the case with fellow employees?

Just something they noticed, but they could be wrong, of course. The staff uniform feels a bit too tight. Can another be supplied, or what about the wage slip that always seems to underpay.

Now time for the codependent people pleasers. Any chance of them swapping shifts, so they work the graveyard Saturday nights instead. Phrased as the narcissist doing them a favor, of course!

As codependents struggle with the words 'No thanks,' this will be well and truly exploited. Helping the narcissist out on tasks at their own expense is another favorite, as is their willingness to participate in car share to and from work. Always their car of course with promised petrol money in a reliably short supply.

What about the gossips, always good to get onside without realizing that the narcissist is spreading as much about them as they are others. 'So and so always seems to spend time in the manager's office' or 'watch out for the guy in delivery they cant be trusted' and 'what about the woman on the machines that seem to cut corners with safety'.

Not that they are out to spread rumors. Pitting two employees against each other is another favorite tactic, and in this respect, the works gossip is an easy target to blame. Easy for someone to believe the source of this misinformation that the narcissist has passed on with only their best interests at heart.

Being larger than life characters, narcissists love attention and will do their utmost through antics or force of personality to ensure this is never in short supply. The more timid of a fellow employee becomes a source of ridicule, and staff meetings are now the place for the narcissist to showcase their vast repertoire of theatrics and debating skills. All for the benefit of everyone in attendance, as here is the new 'Top dog' in the making.

Feet firmly under the table with confidence soaring, the narcissist continues to shift up through the gears. Bullying colleagues through force of personality becomes commonplace.

Consummate actors do have this uncanny ability at making themselves always look busier than they are and, as such, begin to demand special privilege. Decisions are questioned, and the weaker employee begins to defer to the narcissist's instruction bypassing lines of authority. Management becomes undermined, and the more skilled or talented employees start to feel resentful of blatant favoritism now in the making.

Forget punctuality and teamwork. They are now heading out the window along with staff morale with what appears to be one rule for a certain member of staff and another for all the rest.

Time for management to take action, but some are prone to decisiveness. In contrast, others fall prey to the benefit of the doubt, and the narcissist will have weighed up management as being inclined to the latter long before they started their antics.

If perceived as more potent, they would have walked a long time ago. Instead, employees voicing their concerns will now be singled out and targeted as verbal insults are commonplace. The more sensitive decide their services will be best served elsewhere while the remainder sticks it out and either stand up to the bully or suffer in silence.

Management now perceived as weak experience others taking liberties with long breaks or poor timekeeping as what was once a united workforce divides itself into camps.

A rot is now beginning to set in, and the narcissist has achieved their aim, attention-seeking to the last, now at the epicenter of an engineered situation entirely of their own making.

Becoming more disruptive by the day unless perceived as being in control, arguments become commonplace while all the time is playing the victim and acting all innocent with those that carry some clout. A more confident manager will, by this time, see through all the lies, while a lesser mortal will see the narcissist as someone too valuable to lose. 'Just look at how busy they always are'.

With boundaries now being crossed on a regular basis other employees, now justifiably follow suit, and a rot well and truly sinks in with the narcissist leading the way.

Absenteeism gathers apace, and productivity slackens as employees spend more time pitting their wits against each other as they concentrate on the job at hand. Management becomes held up most days in their office dealing with ongoing staff grievances—a perfect situation of the narcissist's own making.

By the time the company finally wakes up to the cause of this seriously disruptive influence, the narcissist has become embedded in the system, fully aware of their rights and only willing to launch grievance procedures at the drop of a hat.

Management now walks a tightrope. Do they try and keep the narcissist onside, aware of the influence they have over their colleagues, or do they take them on, knowing full well if they make the wrong call and slip up with procedure, it will be exploited by the narcissist to the hilt and Head Office will be asking more questions of them than they do the disruptive employee. With mortgages to pay and mouths to feed, most will veer on the side of caution.

By the time it gets to this stage, there are only two options left to be rid of them. The first is to rely on the narcissist slipping up by pushing their luck, which of course, they always do, but that leaves the ball in their court, not the management. The second and preferable option is for someone to show more decisive leadership and take them on.

Underneath all this bravado lies an incredibly anxious individual full of self-doubt and insecurity who engineers disruptive situations always to attract attention and gain control.

Just with relationships, the same criteria applies, decisiveness. Apply boundaries of what will and will not be tolerated, and it has to be followed through. Narcissists always know when the game is up, just a pity for everyone concerned that it took so long to get to this stage.

So if that was what to look forward to with narcissistic employee's what of narcissistic management, and can the two ever work in harmony. The answer, yes, they can, but god helps everyone else. The above was bad enough, but jeez, can you imagine the atmosphere with that scenario. For further insight in this dept see Chapter entitled 'Can narcissists be out narcissised'.

So if they are terrible employees, what are they like as managers? In a nutshell, abysmal, but that then begs the question, so how the hell did they get promoted in the first place? How many times in our lives have we come across these characters who are superb at talking the talk but in reality, that's about as far as it ever goes. Then what do you know?

A few years later, you discover that you have been leapfrogged in the company hierarchy, and this chancer is off and running. How did that happen? Not unsurprisingly, there is no secret, and the reasons are a repeat of everything discussed thus far.

While the majority of competent, indeed talented, hard-working employees may be the most qualified for promotion, they're frequently passed over in favor of their narcissistic counterpart, who has less experience and doesn't seem that brilliant. Why? Because the hardworking employee plays by the rules and the narcissists don't.

Let's get the charisma out of the way. Well, it's always going to be mentioned foremost because they usually have it by the bucket load.

Of course, narcissists who enjoy being the center of attention often make a terrific first impression on clients and new bosses who are partial to the odd bit of flattery. Others might say kissing ass. Being charismatic also helps when pitching their ideas or usually ideas nicked from a more self-effacing counterpart but rebranded as their own.

The outward signs of self-assurance, the mask they wear to cover up their internal feelings of inadequacy, draws others towards them. Having the gift of the gab enhances this image and shows their leadership potential. All a complete act, but as humans, we tend to be drawn to people who feel sure of themselves.

By ordering others around, especially their people-pleasing counterparts, their leadership potential comes to the fore. Note, of course, that they choose their victim. No point in upsetting the image applecart by ordering around a self-confident but probably more modest colleague. These people will just be sucked up to instead.

What about pushiness. Narcissists are always pushy, but it has to be a question of degree in working their way up the ladder. Once they get to the top, they can exercise more bullying behavior, but it has to be controlled in the interim. In this respect, think back to my chapter 'Narcissists and Control' and my run-in with a seriously pushy female colleague.

She was undoubtedly an ambitious character and, to the word, displayed all of the above criteria but her downfall, she just went way overboard with being in your face domineering.

She pushed her luck, couldn't rein it in, and instead of carefully choosing her victim, she just tried to dominate every character she came in contact with. What it boils down to here is that don't assume all narcissists are masters with manipulation. Some need to go on refresher courses to brush up on their skill set.

What out of hours networking. These may be minor events in the early days, but rest assured, the narcissist will be first in line. Always looking a million dollars irrespective of the unpaid bills lying on the doormat, this is the time for the narcissist to hone in on those that matter.

Just as they are adept at giving a subtle critique to their accommodating colleagues, they are masters at providing modest praise to their 'loving every minute of it' superiors.

All bosses like their ego stroked at some point. If a golf day out, watch out for the narcissist suddenly taking lessons and buying the best equipment to keep up. Not wanting to look a fool on the day, a last-minute sprained ankle or tennis elbow may ensue but rest assured, the end-of-day entertainment will never be missed.

Not only do they get to meet their own boss but also their boss's boss. This performance will be prepared for months in advance. I refer back to playing by the rules. Do they rely on their ability at work to do the talking, or is the machiavellian stuff infinitely more preferable and much easier to operate for them? As most successful self-made business people often profess. 'Stick to what you know'.

They finally get to where they want to be, well in as far as just for the time being as still further ladders to climb, and boredom will eventually kick in at some point. Not just relationships that bore narcissists. It's everything. What's the difference between a narcissist as an employee and a narcissist as a manager? In short, not a lot!

As ever, just a question of degree! In some areas, they slacken off, but in others, they beef it up and for this top of the tree is bullying. By being indifferent or verbally abusive to those who don't conform or kiss their ass, these employees are now on a hiding to nothing.

A narcissist will always bear a grudge, and opportunities to settle old scores will be resolved without hesitation. Being criticized is no longer so subtle and expect to be belittled in front of others if the mood takes them or instructions are not followed to the tee.

The other side of the coin is that those who do suck up and carry out every instruction, no matter how stupid, will be singled out for preferential treatment and looked after. In essence, the narcissist's ideal workforce is a team of complete 'yes men'.

All very well being a complete yes man and having an easier life, but it comes with conditions. These are tending to their selfish needs over and above their job description. Expect these people to run personal errands or take on inappropriate chores, pet projects even as part of their unofficial job description, all without proper pay or even the slightest bit of gratitude.

Meetings. Narcissists do like meetings as this is a show-time opportunity and tend to be ever so slightly one-sided. Who does most of the talking? They do this by reminding subordinates of remarkable achievements and why their ideas and suggestions are so much better than everyone else's. Then, heaven help anyone who dares disagree, shot down in flames to mark authority, as well as sending out a signal that dissent in the camp will not be tolerated. These people are then sidelined from further meetings and held in contempt.

Never expect praise from a narcissistic manager. Even the 'yes men' receive at best scant recognition but at least less criticism than everyone else. Narcissists struggle with praise as for them, this displays weakness and could represent future challenges further down the line. As it's all about control, the best and only way the narcissist knows how is to keep everyone under their thumb. Smashing someone's confidence or eroding self-belief are the perfect ways to achieve this.

Not exactly great for team morale, but when did that ever have anything to do with it. Good ideas are stolen, as always, and credit for productivity or sales is given to the arse lickers and out-of-hours personal shoppers. You can imagine how great this must be for staff morale.

Obviously, in the early days, the new manager would have swept everyone off their feet with an outgoing charismatic personality but with all the above beginning to kick in, it does not take that long in the bigger scheme of things for a malaise to envelope the workplace. As discussed earlier, the workplace will be divided into factions on the shop floor, and the narcissistic manager becomes paranoid about who they can trust.

As control is ingrained in their psyche, the 'yes men' give daily feedback about potential dissenters in the camp who will be targeted accordingly with less than subtle criticism or emotional abuse. The trouble with narcissistic managers is that there will always be someone further down the line who has weighed them up, is not easily intimidated, and is smarter than they are. This becomes panic stations.

If the more intelligent employee cannot be bullied and rejects a charm offensive, then there's only one thing for it. Ship them out elsewhere. How often have perfectly settled employees been transferred elsewhere as their skill set is in demand at another branch or depot? Bet your bottom dollar it will not be for a reason given.

In a nutshell, you will not be surprised to hear that even as managers, it is still always about them. Forget about leading a team from the front or anything about collective responsibility.

Narcissism is about dominance, and narcissists make themselves feel better by making others feel small. Whatever it takes, belittling, condescending, critical, or just plain sending a snotty memo or email. For them, it has more to do with feelings of power and authority derived from being abusive than it is worried about the feedback.

If this is narcissistic management at a middle or senior management level, then what about right at the very top, the CEOs of this world. We often look on CEOs as the new rock stars of the noughties. Think back to the financial crash of 2008 and look at the lifestyles, certainly living like one. Corporate jets on standby and fruit being flown halfway across the world for meetings that lasted minutes.

Instead of the rock stars competing for the biggest mansion, think the new breed of CEO on their disastrous acquisition spree, grossly overpaying for companies that still allowed them to be bigger than their nearest competitor but forget about the debt and diminishing share value. Even for a narcissistic CEO, size matters.

What is the difference between a narcissist in middle management and those at the very top of the tree? Honestly, very little, but most behavior now goes unchecked in the latter case, with the CEO now answering to no one. Forget the Chairman, appointed to keep the CEO in line. Do you think they were carefully selected for any other reason than to give their nod of approval occasionally?

In 1978 the average CEO earned 26 times more than the average worker—It's now 210 times more. CEOs of S & P index companies make 354 times more than the average employee. Furthermore, two recent scientific studies confirm what we have always known. Narcissistic CEOs ruin companies by demoralizing and alienating employees and committing corporate fraud, all in the name of self-serving interest.

Many narcissistic leaders are very good at what they do. Their charisma and self-belief in getting the job done allow them to take considerable risks that often pay off. Often with a few successful deals under the belt, a self-serving Midas belief prevails, and their need for self-importance and admiration ultimately gets in the way and proves to be their downfall.

A factor in this is the narcissist's need for total control. CEOs are no different; hence, a new CEO's first strategy is to bring in a loyal band of lieutenants to instigate and protect the implementation of directives. The larger the company, the more crucial it is to have a senior team swearing complete allegiance to the CEO's cause.

This way, the CEO can seal themselves off from lower-level employees with who they have little interest in making contact. Just like the narcissistic manager who surrounds himself with 'yes men,' the CEO is out to do the same. Same principle but significantly different pay rates.

The CEO likes to surround themselves with executives lower in esteem and willing to allow the CEO to take all the credit for positive outcomes. Importantly they will also identify more with the narcissistic CEO than the organization.

CEO's also like to promote younger, more inexperienced people to key positions not because they are less capable but because they will prove to be more loyal through gratitude and obligation. Trust for a narcissist of any persuasion is paramount.

They have control, so what about the attention. No small non-existent headline-making acquisitions for the narcissistic CEO. It has to be big and grab the headlines, preferably resulting in several prime-time interview and photo opportunities. Even the unpleasant decisions can be turned around to advantage. Redundancies, again, make them big, so it makes the main news at least.

The downside to having a boardroom full of compliant non dissenters is that sooner or later, the terrible decisions that went unchallenged come home to roost.

Profit warnings are now de rigeur, and unsavory questions are asked at the AGM. Needless to say, the PR machine spins into overdrive. External pressures are blamed as always alongside that old chestnut, 'drop in sales due to uncertainty in the market'.

When the shit finally does hit the fan, look out for the blame game once more, and the narcissist does what he does best, shift blame left, right, and center onto those more willing subordinates while at the same time playing them off against each other.

Again think back to the early stages of 2008. Blame being apportioned here, there, and everywhere and how they must have hated the public inquiries—finally held up solely accountable for their disastrous stewardship.

To be criticized is bad enough, but to be publicly humiliated, I cannot think of anything more painful for a narcissist. Wonder how many stopped off at the liquor store on their way home that night?

What to do then if working with a narcissist. Well, if you're pretty near the top of the tree earning a few million bucks or more, why not just keep sucking up to them.

For a few million a year, I probably would as well, safe in the consolation that at some point or another, they are going to seriously overpay for a distinctly average competitor or become embroiled in the kind of tabloid loving front-page scandal that their risk-taking behavior deserves. Hang around for long enough, and they will implode. Don't take my word for it. Like I said, history is littered with examples.

Royal Bank of Scotland

HBOS Bank

Northern Rock

Lehman Bros

AIG

Enron

Robert Maxwell

Ratners

Lexmark

Worldcom

Bear Sterns

Swissair

Arthur Anderson

Barings Bank

BCCI

Laker Airways

ZZZZ Best

So that's the fat cats, but what about the rest of us having to work with them. The first part is to identify them. As for me, you know what, I now make my mind up by the end of their first week and usually run with it. For added validation, if narcissistic, they will be on social media, and from that, it becomes clear as daylight if they become dispatched to the 'To be avoided like the plague' danger zone.

For help in this area, see the chapter entitled 'The narcissist and social media'. No computer, then don't worry. Put it this way. If you feel this employee loves attention, talks a good game, always asks for help but never reciprocates, is unreliable, and enjoys subtle criticisms. You know what, chances are they probably are. So don't bother looking for further validation. It's all you need to know.

What does one do then to minimize disruption and still have a comfortable experience at work before a half-decent manager comes along and kicks them into touch or preferably out the door? Here are a few pointers.

- Simple but effective. Just stay in your lane, get on with your job, and don't allow yourself to become distracted. Being known as a conscientious and dependable employee will always prevail and defend you from the mudslinging that will inevitably be thrown your way by the same person trying to chummy up alongside you. If the narcissist asks you for a hand, decline, stating that you have too much work of your own to be getting on with. When they do, put out the feelers to gauge your opinion on fellow employees. Simply state you like to keep your opinions to yourself. In short, keep your distance.

- Do not be taken in by all the flattery. Once they realize you are no soft touch, they will go on a serious charm offensive. If you are held in some esteem by superiors, this just makes you even more appealing.

- At all costs, try and avoid having to go through a narcissist for instruction or information. They are known for sabotaging others and, of course, will deny any wrongdoing on their part. Sometimes you will just have to, but best to double-check with another line manager to be on the safe side.

- Make sure and keep other relationships alive with fellow colleagues and superiors. Being on friendly terms with someone two or three rungs above the narcissist will always stand you in good stead for when they launch a character assassination or simple sabotage as above.

- In short, keep your wits about you at all times. Bear in mind it will always be temporary. Narcissists do not hang around in jobs very long when others are not playing ball.

CHAPTER 14

THE NARCISSIST AND MONEY

You know the type, those euphemistically known in the trade as 'tight' with money, or at least when it comes to paying their share. There are the obvious ones. The friends who suggest in advance to split the bill, then go ahead and order the Fillet while everyone else has settled for the Ribeye. They order a more expensive bottle of wine than if they had been paying for it themselves, and how about an extra pudding. So damn good, just got to have another, and how about a liqueur? Tips all around, but you hand over a note while they rummage around for some loose change.

Work colleagues will gladly take a drink on a Friday night but always seem to disappear to the loo when it's about to be their turn. To give them some credit, at the very least, they are setting out their stall in advance, so you know what to expect the second time around because there will never be a third.

The other year I met up with some friends for a walk in the Scottish Borders. One of the friends was an old University acquaintance I remembered well as he had a reputation for being 'tight'. But now, as a high-flying Chartered Accountant, he must be doing alright for himself.

With his propensity for figures, I wondered if he chose the job or had the job chosen him. Let's call him Gordon, a fairly common name back in 1970's Scotland. Nice three or four-mile walk to work up an appetite, then lunch at a pub renowned for its generous portion sizes. An hour and a half spent either reminiscing or putting the world to rights, and it's time to bid our farewells.

Just time to settle up and guess what? Gordon has come away without his wallet. So from the late Seventies to the present day, in a period just shy of 40 years, Gordon has changed not one iota. Still as 'tight' as ever!

In fact, given his likely earning potential, you could probably say he's now ten times worse. The adage 'If you're looking for someone to change, you're in for a very long wait' did rather spring to mind. Of course, he's full of remorse and repentance, but next time around, 'don't worry,' the drinks will be on him. Needless to say, there was no second time around as I never invited him back.

Now I don't have an issue with people being frugal. More often than not, it is a circumstance that dictates spending power, and we all make allowances for adults working to feed more mouths than the rest of us have to contend with.

The difference with the Gordon's of this world is that they quite clearly take the rest of us as being mugs, and although only an afternoon spent in his company, still enough time to get a 'feeling' about someone and with sufficient experience under my belt by this time I decided to act on instinct. Our paths were never to cross again.

Unlike me, however, my more open-minded friends continued with the memory lane friendship before they too realized that I was right after all. He was worse, and the fact that by outing No 3, he was still being collected and returned to his flat, thus saving on the petrol money just reinforced the fact. It made me feel temporarily smug!

Was I smarter, or perhaps I had more bitter experiences under my belt to draw on. Not that being 'tight' in itself predetermines narcissistic behavior. Still, extreme selfishness does and is a good enough indicator for everyone concerned in this instance to cut their losses in advance of probably worse still to come.

We all use the money to make us feel better about ourselves. Nothing wrong with enjoying the fruits of your hard-earned labors. Used wisely alongside other factors, it can lead to a satisfying and contented life. Used foolishly as per my examples at the beginning of the chapter 'How could I have been so stupid,' it inevitably causes no end of friction or despair.

Whereas the vast majority of us take nothing for granted and use it for the occasional treat, a narcissist believes they are continually entitled to the best even when they quite clearly lack the funds to afford it. Why? 'Because they are worth it.'

With fragile self-esteem, narcissists use the money to make themselves feel unique and more important than others in their peer group. By splashing out on designer clothes, flash cars, exotic holidays, and show homes with bespoke kitchens, they allow themselves an air of superiority over others known to them that they are doing a lot better.

But, as I said before, being a narcissist does not come cheap, so it is a wonder most operate as complete freeloaders to compensate.

There are more anecdotes for your entertainment, but always highlight the complete double standards that seem to pervade their thinking. When we first met my little social media-loving friend, the bulk of her expenditure was met by Welfare.

She led a kind of hand-to-mouth existence with the red reminders arriving on an almost daily basis. Such was the complexity of her personal life; the Police and Social Services were also never far away. I think things happened so often and with such regularity in that little cul de sac of hers that the curtains from across the road no longer twitched. It was just a given when the blue lights came flashing as to why they were here.

Yet for all the nonsense, she had to feel 'better' than those living opposite which, for her, came by way of the car with a badge and designer label clothes. At one stage, even joining the 'oldest profession in order to keep the creditors at bay.

But, for someone who had bags of initiative, it always disappointed me that her skewed approach to money meant that every day for probably the rest of her life would continue to be an uphill battle. Having decent food on the table and a warm house would always come secondary to putting on the show that she was somehow 'better' than everyone else.

Moving up the social scale a notch or two, how about my run-in with a bullying female colleague. The same woman who thought nothing of bragging about her latest foreign holiday or expensive tattoo yet regularly cadged lifts to and from work from colleagues who lived only a few blocks away.

At the same time, her own sports car sat in the driveway. The gestures were never reciprocated, of course, and why blow money on a packet of cigarettes when you can sponge off others before nipping outside for a quick puff. Management's ear would then be regularly bent to allocate lucrative overtime in her direction over her more generous counterparts. Being unchallenged for so long, was it any wonder she thought she was superior?

Then what of Ted? Now he was in a league of his own when it came to spending other people's money. No option really as he had diddly squat of his own, although to listen, you would think his career had been one of unbridled success.

As I said, I met Ted through work, having sold his Book Wholesalers, he had moved into logistics as, you know, it gets kind of boring sitting about the house all day living off the Bank interest, so had gone back to work to alleviate the monotony.

On the face of it, the image matched the story. Large house in the country and latest Red Porsche out front! What's not to think this man's self-made? Scratching the surface, however, revealed a different story.

True, he had been temporarily self-employed, but instead of following Sam Walton's advice that most overnight successes are twenty years in the making, he just went for it and lavished out on all the trappings long before there was sufficient income or an established client base to pay for it.

Ted would have been better employed with Pyramid selling as his financial short-sightedness was a characteristic of which narcissists are notorious.

Always believing that the next big deal is only just around the corner, they spend lavishly long before customers commit. The business imploded, and here he was starting afresh, having declared bankruptcy but in his wake leaving others behind to pick up the pieces of lost revenue. What did he care? He'd had his fun, and here he was using the charm offensive to start all over again. You know the rest.

Now I know one or two successful people, hell by a certain age most of us do and for sure they lead a comfortable life, but apart from that, you can safely say that their lives are for the most part, well, every day. Of course, if they want something that badly, they just go ahead and buy it that bit quicker than the rest of us can manage, but in the main, they strike me as being happy with their lot.

Having made no small amount of sacrifice to achieve their success, I guess that financial short-sightedness is most definitely not a flaw they have to contend with. However, I am also of the opinion that these are the fortunate few who love their jobs where the money has followed on the back of them being so good at what they do in the first place.

For the Teds of this world, you can forget about job satisfaction; it's the money that counts. Having bought into a dud of a Franchise, you could safely bet he was out narcissised by an even smoother talking salesman who recognized a greedy man when he saw one. Ted's eyes would have positively lit up when faced with the opportunity of complete pie in the sky on-target earnings.

Where does it come from? Why this need to feel superior to everyone else, especially when the same peer group eventually sees them as nothing more than complete tits. I mentioned in the Introduction that it was not my intention to explain why narcissists are the way they are, and I don't intend to start now, but for sure, as mentioned, low self-esteem is always evident.

The crucial part is that they have to feel more important to everyone else belonging to the same peer group. Look at my little friend. Having spent a lifetime on Welfare, she can hardly expect to feel superior to those in a higher income bracket, but she sure as hell tried to feel superior to those in the same boat.

Then the two examples stated who was in the more modest income bracket, afforded the luxury of having others to look down on but still living in excess of their income because it provides the kudos of having a lifestyle they believe superior to that of their peers.

Ted liked to boast that if needed, he would sweep streets or wash dishes if ever he fell on hard times but in reality, those kinds of jobs were way beneath a man of his stature and preferred instead to sponge off his elderly father. The latter was responsible for buying the Porsche in the first place and had been paying the rent on the farmhouse since he moved in with his son shortly after. He had to sell his house years earlier to pay off Ted's previous debts.

Narcissists such as Ted have very selective memories when it comes to dealing with their chequered financial history. Unwilling to accept responsibility for their plight, it is usually down to bad luck or external circumstances.

Then what of the Chris's of this world. Decent income but still never enough! Just as we might know one or two people who have done alright for themselves, chances are we probably know a whole load more living a lifestyle where debt likely provides the missing link.

According to a leading UK Insurer, those people who are so far in the red that they have to take out more credit to avoid problems are those you think really should not have to. It found that 30% of those using cards to survive earned between 30K and 70K compared to 25% of people who earned around 15K. Speculation that the Insurer itself attributed to a 'keeping up with the Jones's led phenomenon.

For sure, higher salaries afford much higher credit limits which probably explains the gap, but why this continuing upward trajectory given the fickle state of employment and interest rates so low, which everyone just knows cannot last indefinitely.

Referring back to 'Narcissists and Social Media' for a moment, my point was that although Facebook et al. did not cause narcissism and cannot be blamed in their entirety for its upward path, they still helped in their way to speed along the process.

Ditto, the same principle with ease of credit. Not directly responsible, but it sure helps motor things along. Paired together, they have created this perfect storm of what appears to be an increasing section of middle England jostling to be bigger or better than their counterparts, but at what cost?

With quite literally millions out there, especially joint income earners on high five-figure salaries, even just the thought of being wealthy becomes enough to create feelings of superiority and entitlement. Still, with such a vast swathe of the same demographic in the same position, it becomes harder for the narcissist jockeying for the No 1 position.

Look all around you. Have you ever known a time when there have been so many people having house extensions? You look, and kind of say to yourself, 'But wait a minute, there are only two of you.' What about cars? When have you ever known people change their cars so often as they do nowadays? Justified, of course, by everyone claiming to have been given a great deal, but if my years of experience have taught me anything, it is with finance.

There will only ever be one winner, and it's not you. Then there are the holidays. At one time, going on a Cruise was left to the preserve of the top 5%, but now everyone is getting in on the act. Not just a once-in-a-lifetime cruise, but for many, it has become several times a year. Ever get the impression that people are now competing with who goes the more exclusive holiday.

'Oh, we became a bit tired of cruising. This year will be our third Safari.'

Now there's nothing new about keeping up with the Joneses, but for the malignant narcissists out there aiming to continually be the biggest and the best amongst their peer group, things sure have gotten a hell of a lot harder. Maybe in times previous, they could have got by, just.

But with so many others now in on the 'Aren't I wonderful' act, there's nothing left for it but to just keep upping the ante with more of this and bigger of that, hoping that as many freebies as possible can be scrounged or small tradesmen fobbed off until the whole house of cards comes crashing down which it usually does.

So what then of narcissists at the very top of the tree? Those multi-millionaires or billionaires are able to live like Kings without the worry of meeting the monthly minimum repayments like their more inferior wannabees. Indeed when your salary is in the millions, it removes the petty insecurities of those struggling to compete on just a few hundred grand. Actually, No! Same principle, just different degrees.

Just as there is a narcissistic hierarchy with friends and jobs, the same applies to money.

Looking down on those below with tens of millions less while living in envy of those with the same amount more. The worst part is trying to feel superior to those more or less on an equal footing which is when the lavish spending or excessive risk-taking comes to the fore. Need an example of narcissistic billionaires behavior, then look no further than the London property market.

It's still keeping up with the Joneses but at a level that's now gone completely off the scale. Size matters to narcissists of all incomes where you must just live in the biggest house. More problematic in London, which explains why so many townhouses in Kensington and Chelsea are being converted into one where Ballroom and underground pool come as de rigeur.

If the house and car cannot suffice, then there's always the yacht, of course, and these do sort the men from the boys as status symbols. Most now come with their very own helipad, and a few are known to carry their mini-submarine as a playful accessory.

But, for sure, be it Cannes, Monte Carlos, or St Tropez, there's no danger of the narcissist just berthing up alongside. More like anchoring up at the most desirable spot for everyone to see, in particular the paparazzi who will have been tipped off long before arrival screaming, 'Look at me, look at me!'

It was the narcissistic Billionaire American socialite Leona Helmsley, dubbed the Queen of Mean. She famously said 'Only little people pay taxes' prior to her being jailed for eighteen months in 1989 for tax evasion, and her behavior typifies that of the narcissistic billionaire.

Eager to flaunt their wealth when it suits but penny-pinching and almost tyrannical to those inferior little people in their employment below. Businesses will be bought at the drop of a hat with thousands paid off under the guise of efficiency savings, all the while the fat cat salts away the proceeds in one of their many offshore accounts.

For those unfortunate multi-millionaire narcissists still classed as employees being mere CEOs, always the opportunity to have the best of both worlds. Again look back no further than the 2008 UK banking crash. Not only did they have the opportunity to write their multi-million-pound paycheques virtually, but they more or less decided their multi-million-pound bonuses into the bargain.

Were these amounts agreed on what was deemed the fair going rate or more than likely see what their nearest competitor earns and then add 20%. Is it any wonder when behavior such as this is tolerated that people begin to believe they are untouchable?

Remember how they all basked in the adoration of orchestrating the latest multi-billion pound acquisition. Still, when the shit finally hit the fan a short while later, they cited unforeseeable circumstances beyond their control. Commonly known as wanting their cake and eat it.

Narcissists of all social denominations are obsessed with money as with enough of it, will mask other inadequacies bubbling under the surface of their lives. For sure, just as I know one or two well-off people in my little sphere who choose not to flaunt it, there will be dozens more who prefer a more low-key approach for every narcissistic person who is utterly minted and from this parting tale springs to mind.

Some fantastically wealthy family, but as normal as can be when you are incredibly wealthy, had advertised for a Butler as the existing one of many years had retired and gone off to grow Tomatoes in his twilight years. So anyway, a new one with impeccable credentials was employed as this guy had worked for the best and most famous of them all, so he knew the ropes inside out. The trouble was, this family was not his mainstream client.

They did not go to showbiz parties, and they did not spend weekends flying off in their private jet, taking him in tow and heavens above.

When the rich guy was not working, they liked to sit down as a family and watch TV. He was even known to get his 'Ride-on' mower out of the garage and mow the lawn on the weekend. How dull is that for a billionaire? The family did not ditch the Butler. He ditched them! It seems the new employee had more of a thing about being seen in all the right places than they had.

For some narcissists, maybe it's not about the money after all!

CHAPTER 15

RED FLAGS – SOUND FAMILIAR?

If narcissists have one redeeming quality, and I use that term loosely, it is their predictability. Once you learn the format, it will never change irrespective of who the particular narcissist may be. Work colleague, romantic partner, friend, or neighbor, it matters not a jot. The script remains the same, which in their dealings is to bear in mind the following.

Never take anything at face value. Things are never as they seem.

Promises made will never be kept.

Expect to be taken for granted, and crucially, whatever passes from between their lips should be taken with a pinch of salt.

Narcissist spotting to me is akin to learning to swim or riding a bike. At some point, it just 'clicks', and before you know it, everything just falls into place. They now just seem to stand out a hell of a lot more, walking around as if there is a giant red arrow above their head, firmly pointing downwards. Pity we all have to go through so much shit to get to this stage but think of the potential heartache saved in the future. Think no pain, no gain.

No lengthy academic research was conducted with the following. Simply my observations, most of which I tried my best to incorporate into Sarah's story. Some have since sprung to mind in the course of writing. No doubt you will have some favorites of your own, and if you want to share, please feel free and pass them on. You can get me at 'tryandavoidnarcsliketheplague.com'

See if any of the following resonate?

Narcissists are masters of the great first impression. Initial attention was gained through their looks but polished off with what seems like effortless charm and charisma. The conversation appears natural, never stilted or contrived. Almost immediately, you feel at ease. This has not happened by accident.

The same amount of time will have been devoted to learning their craft as mastering a sport or musical instrument. Endless hours spent in front of the bathroom mirror perfecting the smile, the laugh, or the opening line.

Their likes and dislikes appear to mirror your own. Mainly because they allow you to make, the first move being somewhat non-committal themselves in early dialogue. As most people have fairly standard mainstream interests, this can quickly be capitalized on when the time comes to take the conversation further. Thinking on their feet is in a narcissist's DNA.

Job titles are always grandiose while at the same time feigning modesty. Guess they were in the right place at the right time, but the place would now just go to pieces if they left. If self-employed, they can't believe how busy they are. Just can't keep up with demand etc. etc. Offers to buy out business but still too young to retire!

They do like attention. Every available photo opportunity is taken advantage of. A group photo wants to be center stage; being on the periphery just won't do. If unable to be center, then making some gesture or act to make them stand out from everyone else will be called upon.

They like to make an entrance at any social event and usually have a band of merry followers in tow, laughing the loudest at the most average of jokes. These people have been courted for their insecurity and need to belong.

They do have a thing about the image, and brand names come as de rigeur for a narcissist. Part of the feigned modesty is to avoid mentioning the designer label or Rolex but, on the other hand doing everything they possibly can to make sure the status emblem is seen. This will have been perfected in front of the mirror at home; see point above.

The car and the house are, of course, the ultimate status symbols. Never mind that they are mortgaged to the hilt [interest only], or the cars are never owned outright as long as the image suits, then the stress of remortgaging or juggling balance transfers makes it all worthwhile. A credit check will almost always blow a hole in the narcissist's self-image.

Pretentious coffee table books of the black and white variety will always be strategically on show. The bookcase will also have its fair share of, as yet, unopened literature of the pseudo-intellectual variety.

Personalized number plates come as standard for a narcissist but so does driving around endlessly looking for the cheapest fuel on offer. Those loyalty cards saving derisory amounts will be hidden in the glove compartment or under the seat.

Narcissists love social media. Endless hours spent choosing the perfect photoshopped image of them and their new partner professing undying love. 'Soul mate' and 'the partner I have been waiting for all my life' will be sold for all the world to see.

Their personal lives always appear complicated. Children by one or more partners are not uncommon. Their exes are denounced as crazy in some shape or form, forcing the end of the relationship, which they so bravely attempted to save.

They will have become estranged from parents or fellow siblings. Never their fault, of course! If you ever get to meet some of these relatives, you will find they bear little resemblance to the picture painted.

You will have been wined and dined at exclusive restaurants or hotels in the early days [watch how they paid— was it by credit card?]. Finding fault is not uncommon, as this will probably result in a reduced bill. The art of complaint will also have been perfected. Name dropping with the manager about who they are or how they intended to return with a larger group of friends will inevitably induce some discount.

From the halcyon days of fine dining comes the reality of bargain-basement cheap deals, now done on a 50/50 basis. Again finding fault is not uncommon for the same discounted net result. Narcissists have no shame when it comes to complaining.

How many times do you remember your narcissist partner saying 'I promise', but somehow the promises never quite came to fruition?

There is no chance of escaping the building society, finance company, or utility bills, but everyone else can wait. Forget about paying the window cleaner, gardener, or corner shop paper bill.

These people are all deemed inferior, as anyone working in service industries, and will be treated accordingly. Working in manual labor is a strict taboo for a narcissist, irrespective of whether these hard-working people play by the rules and don't.

After a couple of months, you will have become aware that the words narcissist and hypocrite go hand in hand.

From being charming and considerate, they have become selfish, moody, and sulky. This is, of course, part of the Testing Phase [see Chapter 2] to see just how far they can push their luck.

From being placed on a pedestal, you now find yourself being criticized for the most inconsequential things. Furthermore, you learn that shrugging the insults off is easier as opposing can induce massive three-week sulks.

At home, they watch endless hours of crap TV [in silence]. Although to be fair, if you spent every working day being someone else, you would want some downtime too.

Their own needs always come first. Your free time has now become their time, and the role of unpaid skivvy ensues.

You notice their intense jealousy of others. Next door neighbor gets a new car. They get a new car. A friend buys a bigger house. Then it's time they also moved on. Other people's success is belittled or put down to luck. Never mind that the majority work ferociously hard or make a tremendous sacrifice. Nothing for a narcissist is ever deemed fair unless in their favor, of course.

As for the inevitable cheating, all very predictable, not their fault. Of course, you drove them to it. You stopped being attentive as if you never cared. Never said 'I love you' anymore. Of course, they were always the dream partner, right??

Not an exhaustive list, there could have been so much more but enough to give the general gist. All about them, always, always, always. If you don't play by their rules, you are history, and if you do, well, you still get shafted anyway, so what's to lose? Even if just a smidgeon of these character traits in your new partner, then buy a goddamn horse and head for the hills.

CHAPTER 16

RECOVERING FROM A NARCISSIST

Moving on from heartbreak is never easy at the best of times. Still, when a narcissist is added to the equation, it fully deserves its remit of a completely soul-destroying experience.

No wonder I was determined to have the word 'torture' in the book title at all costs. It would be great if there were a short-term cure. But, as yet, the only medicine that appears remotely effective is the passing of time.

The worst part about being dumped by a narcissist is that they always leave you with the hope to think you might still be in with a fighting chance when the evidence quite clearly proves to the contrary—commonly known as hedging their bets!

Thinking that if you try just that little bit harder, they will come to their senses is to leave yourself wide open to further abuse and manipulation when they get bored further down the line. You need to ask yourself what this kind of behavior says about them as a person, let alone a partner. Your brain already knows this, but your heart is still lagging some way behind.

I don't claim the following to be a foolproof guide to recovery. But, if it helps over time, at some stage, a little switch will flick in the psyche where they no longer seem of relevance. We all want to get to this stage. If only one of these helps, at least it is a step in the right direction.

ACCEPT IT WAS NEVER A LONG-TERM BET!

Sure there were great times. You had such fun, they were attractive, and you just seemed to 'click' in every way. Now get real! It doesn't take a narcissist long to reveal their true colors, so ask yourself—did you find them moody? Were they selfish? How about control? Were they always keen to know where you were and what you were doing? Were they full of compliments in the early days but becoming more critical as the relationship progressed? Were they full of promises which never quite seemed to materialize?

Now ask yourself if this person was real relationship material. The very fact their track record was so sketchy explains why you find yourself in the same predicament as others have gone before. They just cannot commit!!

Suppose the relationship ended without a clear explanation [and they usually do], then it's up to you to do the figuring out. By understanding why the relationship dissolved, we allow ourselves to end any hopes of reconciliation and move forward with our lives.

STOP BLAMING YOURSELF!

Self-esteem takes a pasting with rejection. That's perfectly understandable, but blaming yourself can make it harder to move on. While it is normal to mull over everything you did wrong, giving in to negative thoughts more than is necessary can hinder or sabotage our capacity to move on.

When two or more of your friends are actually making the same points post-relationship, but we still have difficulty accepting it, we need to consider that they are most likely telling us the truth and understand why we have difficulty accepting it.

The underlying reason is probably one of low self-esteem. For example, the time you started 'bigging yourself up' and taking on some new interests. Sure, you won't find your niche straight away, but no one ever got anywhere without a certain degree of perseverance.

SOCIAL MEDIA STALKING

I just couldn't help myself. Much as I wanted to hit the 'Unfriend' button, I just lacked the guts to do it. The more I played Detective, the worse I felt. Now you may be mentally stronger than I am, in which case you have my admiration. But in the meantime, here's how I coped.

For sure, in the early days, I must have hit their Profile page dozens of times a day, but then, just like an addict, I attempted to wean myself off the 20 times a day Facebook fix. I put a chart up on the wall, and every time I clicked on their profile, I would place a 'tick' against their name and have a daily total.

The challenge was to try and have a reduced score each week. Sometimes it was just a couple, but through time the scores dramatically reduced to the extent the chart was no longer required.

This was just my system, and you can develop your own. But it is a need that has to be overcome. The occasional glimpse is terrific, and at some stage, it becomes positively enlightening further down the line.

TALK THEM OUT OF YOUR SYSTEM!

Talk about this person to anyone prepared to lend an ear. No doubt your friends and family will be bored to tears and will roll their eyes in anticipation of what's about to be said, but who cares. Talk and talk and talk until you begin to bore yourself talking about your ex.

Don't fret too much afterward about having divulged more than you would have liked. People have short memories at the best of times, and more often than not, they would also have been in your shoes at some time in their lives. I talked about my narcissistic ex so much I began to bore myself. When this happens, you are making much more progress than you think!

GIVE YOURSELF A PROJECT

The house is always an easy place to start. Anything that gets you up and gets you active. Something about physical activity with a bit of music in the background makes the day feel that little bit more productive. Sure the worst part is getting started.

But once committed and the first bit of wallpaper has been peeled, there's no going back. You then HAVE to finish the job, and you'll feel a whole load better for it. A more positive distraction than hitting the dating websites listening to other's tales of woe!

Don't rule out exercise. Not only will you feel better, but you'll also look better too.

Get out into nature. Be it a beach, a hill, or a country walk. It will use up your time, and you will come home the better for it. The fresh air sure helps us sleep.

LOOK UP OLD FRIENDS

Those very people that made you feel good just by being in their company. Give them a call. I'll bet you'll make their day just by lifting the phone or dropping an email. No need to worry about making an invite, as I'll bet they beat you to it.

Like I said, this list is hardly exhaustive, and it's all just common sense. But in the early days, easier said than done. Heartbreak must be one of the worst experiences possible, and most of us will have gone through it at some point in our lives. The important point to remember is that, like most things, it will pass.

Once you have gone cold turkey, and with a bit of momentum under your belt, you will be surprised just how soon you get to a position of telling yourself, 'I can't believe I just did that. How could I have been so stupid?'

By then, you may be in a position to contemplate writing your first book!

CHAPTER 17

SO WHAT BECAME OF CHRIS?

Realizing that Sarah's ex Tom was probably a man of his word, any further intrusions into her private life could have repercussions beyond mere superficial injury. Time he finally gave up the ghost and moved on. Besides, more pressing matters now to contend with.

By way of creditors, the vultures were circling overhead, ready to cherry-pick what little assets he had left. Not for the first time, and by now, water off a duck's back to a man of his experience. The closer they get to the precipice, the strategy will always be the same for a narcissist. It's time he raised his game and bought some time.

Current partner Jane now stored on his i-phone under the pseudonym 'Plain' was already in the bag. More of the stay-at-home rather than head-turning variety she would suffice for the time being, and besides, right this moment, beggars can't be choosers.

She made her cheating ex-partner out to be a carbon copy of Chris which he found mildly amusing considering the probable outcome. Who was he to argue with her dependency issues but at least that Saturday night leg over's taken care of, and boy, what a cook!

As for his debts, it was now time to bite the bullet and go for an IVA. There was little alternative, already remortgaged to the hilt and his solitary pension provision with his mother's house. At least IVA's have become so commonplace that they attract little attention in the local classifieds.

No way on earth could he face his name appearing in the Bankruptcy column lest giving these bastards down the Golf Club a field day with his fall from grace. He knew rumors had already been circulating since the change in the car to a more mainstream variety, and the invites are now no longer what they once were.

For a narcissist such as Chris, that can hurt. An online bucket shop lawyer can take care of the finer details while going on the road networking.

Unfortunately, being on the wrong side of forty-five and now on less than 40K is doing absolutely nothing for his street cred. Personal Loan Finance is currently best suited to those facing retirement rather than being in their prime. He had become complacent, as narcissists always do, but things are about to change.

So much for networking being the answer to his prayers. Most contacts proved unavailable, with the majority no longer returning calls. Two even had the audacity to hang up when he finally got through. What little response there was now belonged to the 'Love to help...but' variety.

'After everything he had done for them. The wankers.'

A lifeline by way of his current employer. In essence, his boss wanting a shot of him without the indignity of having to go through a tribunal. Equity release was now back on track after a good few years of hellish publicity, and a new Sales Director has been created to spearhead growth. Would he be interested? Same salary but great commission on much larger amounts.

Forget about crappy five grand loans for a bathroom. We're talking amounts of fifty grand upwards with 5% going into the agent's monthly payslip. Knowing that Chris would probably salivate at the prospect, he gave him the most glowing recommendation while knowing only too well he could turn up the Warp Factor 10 charm offensive at the interview. Fait accompli!

A little bit of flattery can get you anywhere, and for his Interviewer, the charm offensive worked a blinder. This guy's a real pro, he thought to himself after sharing a drink afterward, and what a star Chris proved to be. Having more lives than a cat, Chris was finally back in business.

With cash-strapped pensioners now doing what they can to make ends meet, the relaunch could not have happened at a better time. In the first year alone, the department realizes 1.4 million, of which Chris is personally responsible for 400K. Not bad for a first year's work and with 5% commission, a nice little bonus on top of his salary.

Being temporarily sensible, he clears some debts and now treats plain Jane to a half-decent holiday. By year two, the dept has realized an additional 3 million quid, of which Chris has contributed just shy of a third. Again, a bonus on top of his bonus and a salary increase to match The Chris of old is back, but so are some of the bad behaviors that have been kept in check. His roving eye the first and his arrogance the second. Neither goes unnoticed, but this time around its age, that will ultimately prove to be his nemesis.

Now on year three, targets are smashed as they flog every conceivable policy alongside giving homeowners some much-needed cash: funeral coverage and life insurance sold alongside in the same breath. With Chris's charm, he could sell snow to the Eskimos if it were required, and his team below are expected to produce similar results or face his increasing wrath.

Nonetheless, the revenue keeps pouring in, and at the annual Xmas awards ceremony, he steals the show-winning Sales Manager of the year. Having fobbed off plain Jane that it was employees only, he can now relax, basking in the award-winning adulation as well as try his luck with any female colleagues willing to seek his advice. But, unknown to Chris, tonight was the very long beginning to a concise end.

They had already made their acquaintance a good hour beforehand. Pre-meal drinks where everyone stands in a circle making polite small talk waiting for the alcohol to kick in. Enough time for each other's eyes to register their interest and for her to admit afterward that for a man of his age, he was still a bit of a dish. 'Tread carefully if I was you,' replied the voice of experience.

'Chris Noble can make the best of them look shy and retiring.'

Not that she's going to let slip that was part of his appeal. Never short of male attention, she's always had this thing about older men. That inner confidence, comfortable in their skin, and a touch of arrogance to round things off. Her recent partner for sure was better looking but had zero self-belief, so she called time on that one long before the worrying overtures. Nevertheless, Chris could be of use, and tonight she knew he'd come calling. Hell, she gave him enough signals.

He had been keeping his eye out ever since. No ring on the finger and crucially no partner for the evening. Not that that would have prevented him from trying, it just makes life that little bit easier. So now that the awards are out the way, with his speech easily having been tonight's highlight, he's off in search of Amanda.

Probably a decade younger, but her eyes were positively screaming, come and get me. Two prizes in one night would be rather nice. Abruptly ending his conversation as she deliberately maneuvered to within eyeshot, the chemistry was immediate, although still astute enough to pick up on his insecurities with his prize-winning speech.

Maybe Chris has his flaws after all? Only one way to find out. Playing harder to get than she had initially intended, the best he can manage is her mobile and will be left dangling for a few days before she replies—time enough for his partner to notice a change.

It is the inevitable affair, but this time around, it's Amanda that's now playing hardball. She wants commitment and expects a lifestyle commensurate with a man of his means. Just to prove it, when Chris starts playing for a time, she backs off before finally calling it quits. Just to rub salt in the wound, Jane has now finally woken up and calls time on their relationship before heading back to the internet, searching for a more trustworthy mate. He can wait, but he'd better be patient because his preferred partner will not be coming back anytime soon.

The phone calls go unanswered, and her Testing period has begun. At one point, he's even tempted to call Sarah for advice were it not for the thought of Tom's fist slowly sinking down his throat.

Several days pass by and not a squeak, and she's not to be seen at work either. Chris becomes increasingly volatile at work, with Human Resources alerted to his short temper tantrums. Where the fuck is she, and can he not see what everyone takes as the bleeding obvious.

'You're being played, mate!!'

Still, time to make him sweat a bit yet as he ups the ante with the kind of flowers that go way beyond anything seen at a Supermarket entrance. He likes Amanda. Hell, he's as close as is to falling in love with the woman. No one else in recent years has come remotely close to her confidence, swagger, or attitude. The ladies loos are now a hotbed of gossip.

If this were her stab at Method Acting, then even De Niro would likely have been impressed. But, instead, 'Confused', 'Unsure of his feelings,' 'Did he want a relationship after all?' Complete bollocks can be a winning combination when mixed with sufficient tears, and Amanda has played a winning hand.

Now calling the shots, she will be on fire in the bedroom for the first few weeks, then slowly slip up through the gears. A Caribbean holiday will be on the agenda in the short term, and if they are going to move in together, then one of the new Riverside apartments would go down a treat.

Back to dining out at least three times a week, every other weekend away, and best of all, finally able to show off Amanda at the Golf club. Worth the membership fee alone, even if it's always paid on plastic. Back in the big time, he deliberately parks the new Merc in the Captain's Reserved space just as a statement and works the clubhouse to a tee, all the while his new leggy companion lovingly alongside.

Unfortunately, Chris is no longer as young as he used to be, and things are catching up. Having a partner like Amanda can be an expensive business, and the targets at work continue to be met only by putting in the hours.

His drinking is on the rise, and the odd night he manages to stay at his place can be spent chain-smoking his way through the Duty Frees. His diet is not great, he takes no exercise, and sleep has become increasingly erratic.

Something is going to give, and Amanda is doing her best to encourage that, but he's hooked on her, and she's an addiction that's not going away anytime time soon.

For Sarah, Claire, and plain Jane stalking his Facebook page, there must be a degree of schadenfreud considering how old he now looks compared to his much younger partner, and what's this with the hair dye and tight clothing?

The Riverside apartment comes at a hefty price which does nothing for his stress levels or angina. The only way to be afforded is his mother selling up, which releases the much-needed cash for her spoiled son, and she will then move into his own heavily mortgaged place until she kicks it, and then he can flog that on as well. It's the only way he will manage to buy this apartment, and Amanda sure has her heart set on it.

With the silent treatment, every time he poo poo's the idea, he goes ahead. Joint names, of course, and there's the holiday in between removal dates by way of double celebration. That was just about as good as it ever got, and as the bonuses dried up, so did her interest.

With a female narcissist, they can be even more brutal. At least the male equivalent has the decency to stretch things out a bit by fucking about.

As far as anyone is aware, he's now back home. Still, he has had to sell up lock, stock, and barrel with his mother to keep the wolf from the door and give Amanda her cut.

Realizing that he was now a spent force at work when the offer of Voluntary redundancy finally came along, it was snapped up tout suite as there were now hungrier, better looking, and funnier young Turks snapping at his heels. The general perception was that he had become a bit stale of late by being a dinosaur and one-trick pony. Amanda, too embarrassed with her guilt by association, had gone off to work elsewhere.

What of the other characters in this sorry tale?

Well, Jane met a lovely man on the internet called Tom. Nice, caring man of the gentle giant variety, and what a small world it proved to be. Still, on excellent terms with his ex, the two women have become friends given their unfortunate experience, although the omens are good in the early days.

Elaine is now in a long-term relationship with a partner she met through counseling. The complete antithesis to Chris, he is generous, kind, and caring. However, having had a decade of living with someone so controlling, this has become a whole new experience.

As for Claire, she got off lightly. Her brief infidelity with super snake oil salesman Chris could have been disastrous, but sanity prevailed after. Without realizing it at the time, Sarah had proven to be her savior.

With guys like Chris Noble, it's all about the conquest. The quick fix to be had before moving onto their next vulnerable victim, and so the cycle repeats itself!

It was a valuable lesson for someone still relatively young, so it was quickly snapped up when the marriage proposal came calling a short while later. It did cross her mind to confess and be relieved of her guilt but, with nothing on paper, perhaps the kind of secret best kept hidden.

For Amanda, the trajectory would be more of the same. So why change a winning formula? Snare them, kick into touch and then just move on when the routine becomes boring or monotonous. Either too foolish or arrogant to have learned anything from her aging equivalent, the consequences will inevitably lead to one of enormous personal disappointment.

Having come through the other end, one could easily forgive Sarah for putting relationships on hold for the time being, and now time to pursue interests elsewhere. Bereft of knowledge when Chris was at his most devious and manipulative, it seemed only logical that she put pen to paper and write a book on the subject.

More of the 'stop taking shit' than self-help genre, she must have touched a few nerves as sales were sufficient to warrant a second book, and at the time of writing, she's now on her third. Having packed in the day job a while back, at long last some personal fulfillment albeit in a different way than originally intended!

Having observed her mother's experience, Daughter Becky gained the qualifications necessary to go to University, where she's now on year three of her law degree to enter Family law helping victims of domestic abuse.

But what of the main protagonist? Ostracised by friends and family, what little solace there was usually came by way of alcohol. 'He always had it coming' appeared to be the consensus as for any other information.

No one knows. No one cares!

OTHER BOOKS BY THE AUTHOR

POWER TO THE PEOPLE

PREPARED TO BE TORTURED: THE PRICE YOU WILL
PAY FOR MARRYING A NARCISSIST

Printed in Great Britain
by Amazon

68525938R00139